Enhancing the Climate Resilience of Africa's Infrastructure

Enhancing the Climate Resilience of Africa's Infrastructure

The Power and Water Sectors

Raffaello Cervigni, Rikard Liden, James E. Neumann, and Kenneth M. Strzepek

Editors

A copublication of the Agence Française de Développement and the World Bank

ISBN: 978-1-4648-0466-3
eISBN: 978-1-4648-0467-0
DOI: 10.1596/978-1-4648-0466-3

Cover layout: Critical Stages

Cover photo: ©Wolfgang Steiner. Used with permission of Wolfgang Steiner/Getty Images. Further permission required for reuse.

Library of Congress Cataloging-in-Publication data has been applied for.

Africa Development Forum Series

The Africa Development Forum Series was created in 2009 to focus on issues of significant relevance to Sub-Saharan Africa's social and economic development. Its aim is both to record the state of the art on a specific topic and to contribute to ongoing local, regional, and global policy debates. It is designed specifically to provide practitioners, scholars, and students with the most up-to-date research results while highlighting the promise, challenges, and opportunities that exist on the continent.

The series is sponsored by the Agence Française de Développement and the World Bank. The manuscripts chosen for publication represent the highest quality in each institution and have been selected for their relevance to the development agenda. Working together with a shared sense of mission and interdisciplinary purpose, the two institutions are committed to a common search for new insights and new ways of analyzing the development realities of the Sub-Saharan Africa region.

Advisory Committee Members

Agence Française de Développement
Jean-Yves Grosclaude, Director of Strategy
Alain Henry, Director of Research
Guillaume de Saint Phalle, Head of Research and Publishing Division
Cyrille Bellier, Head of the Economic and Social Research Unit

World Bank
Francisco H. G. Ferreira, Chief Economist, Africa Region
Richard Damania, Lead Economist, Africa Region
Stephen McGroarty, Executive Editor, Publishing and Knowledge Division
Carlos Rossel, Publisher

Sub-Saharan Africa

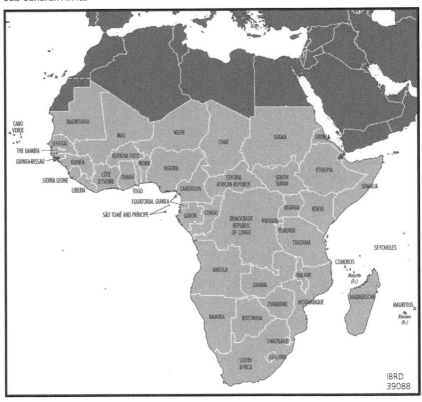

CABO VERDE

MAURITANIA

SENEGAL
THE GAMBIA
GUINEA-BISSAU
GUINEA
SIERRA LEONE
LIBERIA

MALI

BURKINA FASO
BENIN
CÔTE D'IVOIRE
GHANA
TOGO

NIGER

NIGERIA

CHAD

CAMEROON

EQUATORIAL GUINEA
SÃO TOMÉ AND PRÍNCIPE
GABON
CONGO

CENTRAL AFRICAN REPUBLIC

DEMOCRATIC REPUBLIC OF CONGO

SUDAN

SOUTH SUDAN

UGANDA
RWANDA
BURUNDI
TANZANIA

ERITREA

ETHIOPIA

SOMALIA

KENYA

SEYCHELLES

COMOROS
Mayotte (Fr.)

ANGOLA

ZAMBIA

MALAWI

ZIMBABWE
MOZAMBIQUE

MADAGASCAR

MAURITIUS
Réunion (Fr.)

NAMIBIA
BOTSWANA

SWAZILAND

SOUTH AFRICA

LESOTHO

IBRD
39088

Titles in the Africa Development Forum Series

Africa's Infrastructure: A Time for Transformation (2010) edited by Vivien Foster and Cecilia Briceño-Garmendia

Gender Disparities in Africa's Labor Market (2010) edited by Jorge Saba Arbache, Alexandre Kolev, and Ewa Filipiak

Challenges for African Agriculture (2010) edited *by Jean-Claude Deveze*

Contemporary Migration to South Africa: A Regional Development Issue (2011) edited by Aurelia Segatti and Loren Landau

Light Manufacturing in Africa: Targeted Policies to Enhance Private Investment and Create Jobs (2012) by Hinh T. Dinh, Vincent Palmade, Vandana Chandra, and Frances Cossar

Informal Sector in Francophone Africa: Firm Size, Productivity, and Institutions (2012) by Nancy Benjamin and Ahmadou Aly Mbaye

Financing Africa's Cities: The Imperative of Local Investment (2012) by Thierry Paulais

Structural Transformation and Rural Change Revisited: Challenges for Late Developing Countries in a Globalizing World (2012) by Bruno Losch, Sandrine Fréguin-Gresh, and Eric Thomas White

The Political Economy of Decentralization in Sub-Saharan Africa: A New Implementation Model (2013) edited by Bernard Dafflon and Thierry Madiès

Empowering Women: Legal Rights and Economic Opportunities in Africa (2013) by Mary Hallward-Driemeier and Tazeen Hasan

Enterprising Women: Expanding Economic Opportunities in Africa (2013) by Mary Hallward-Driemeier

Safety Nets in Africa: Effective Mechanisms to Reach the Poor and Most Vulnerable (2015) edited by Carlo del Ninno and Bradford Mills

Urban Labor Markets in Sub-Saharan Africa (2013) edited by Philippe De Vreyer and François Roubaud

Securing Africa's Land for Shared Prosperity: A Program to Scale Up Reforms and Investments (2013) by Frank F. K. Byamugisha

Youth Employment in Sub-Saharan Africa (2014) by Deon Filmer and Louis Fox

Tourism in Africa: Harnessing Tourism for Growth and Improved Livelihoods (2014) by Iain Christie, Eneida Fernandes, Hannah Messerli, and Louise Twining-Ward

Land Delivery Systems in West African Cities: The Example of Bamako, Mali (2015) by Alain Durand-Lasserve, Maÿlis Durand-Lasserve, and Harris Selod

The Challenge of Stability and Security in West Africa (2015) by Alexandre Marc, Neelam Verjee, and Stephen Mogaka

Enhancing the Climate Resilience of Africa's Infrastructure: The Power and Water Sectors (2015) edited by Raffaello Cervigni, Rikard Liden, James E. Neumann, and Kenneth M. Strzepek

Africa's Demographic Transition: Dividend or Disaster? (2015) edited by David Canning, Sangeeta Raja, and Abdo S. Yazbeck

All books in the Africa Development Forum series are available for free at https://openknowledge.worldbank.org/handle/10986/2150

Contents

The following appendixes are available online at https://openknowledge
.worldbank.org/handle/10986/21875

A   PIDA+ Infrastructure Plans by Basin

B   Perfect Foresight Adaptation Modeling Methodology

C   WEAP Model

   C1   WEAP General Modeling Approach

   C2   The Congo River Basin

   C3   The Niger River Basin

   C4   The Nile River Basin

   C5   The Upper Orange River Basin

   C6   The Senegal River Basin

   C7   The Volta River Basin

   C8   The Zambezi River Basin

D   OSeMOSYS Model

   D1   OSeMOSYS Common Modeling Assumptions

   D2   The Southern African Power Pool

   D3   The Eastern Africa Power Pool

   D4   The West African Power Pool

   D5   The Central Africa Power Pool

E   Climate Scenarios and Representative Climates

F   Robust Decision-Making Approach

G Data Used as Inputs to the Analysis

Foreword

Understanding the causes and addressing the effects of climate change are central to our efforts to end poverty. The reason is simple: If left unchecked, climate change could potentially overwhelm existing development efforts. Taking the challenge seriously requires a broad focus on its impacts as well as the continued viability of clean, renewable energy sources, many of which—such as hydropower, wind, and solar—are potentially sensitive to climate change even as they are part of the solution.

Nowhere is this more important than in Sub-Saharan Africa, a region that is responsible for a small share of global greenhouse gas emissions, but whose people bear a disproportionate share of the devastating effects of more extreme climate patterns. The good news is that Africa has the ability to manage the effects of climate change and build resilience. One response to these challenges, and one that is essential to Africa's continued economic development, has been to enhance infrastructure, particularly for the water and power sectors. For example, Africa has a large untapped hydropower potential, and it has been estimated to exploit less than 10 percent of its technical potential, the lowest proportion of any of the world's regions.

Yet one of the essential values of infrastructure, its long life span, can make it all the more vulnerable to climate variability. How do we design and build the essential infrastructure needed for Africa's development, while factoring in and addressing the challenge of climate resilience? This book tackles that challenge head on, by sorting complex and uncertain climate science, quantifying the range of climate vulnerabilities of infrastructure performance, and proposing a practical response to these vulnerabilities through careful infrastructure planning and design.

The comprehensive nature of the results—covering seven major river basins and all four of Sub-Saharan Africa's electric power pools—using a unified methodology and dataset, make this a uniquely useful study. But the real power of this volume is in the way it connects directly to institutions engaged in infrastructure investment and climate resilience actions, notably the African Union Commission and its New Partnership for Africa's Development (NEPAD) framework; the UN's Economic Commission for Africa and its African Climate Policy Centre; and the array of river basin authorities and electric power pools. Drawing on the nexus of science, economics, policy, and infrastructure design can help us to harness the growing interest in the impact of climate change on Sub-Saharan Africa and thereby achieve the twin goals of development and climate resilience.

Makhtar Diop
Vice President, Africa Region
The World Bank

Acknowledgments

This volume in the Africa Development Forum series is part of the African Regional Studies Program, an initiative of the Africa Region Vice Presidency at the World Bank. These studies aim to combine high levels of analytical rigor and policy relevance and to apply them to various topics important for the social and economic development of Sub-Saharan Africa. Quality control and oversight are provided by the Office of the Chief Economist for the Africa Region.

The work has been undertaken in collaboration with the African Climate Policy Centre (ACPC) of the United Nations Economic Commission for Africa (UNECA). The ACPC team included Fatima Denton (director, Special Initiatives Division at UNECA), Youba Sokona (former ACPC coordinator), Linus Mofor, Wilfran Moufouma Okia, Joseph Intsiful, and Seleshi Bekele. We also acknowledge input provided by the African Union Commission, in particular, the comments provided by Haruna Gujba and Philippe Niyongabo.

The World Bank task team was led by Raffaello Cervigni and included Vivien Foster (former co–task team leader), David Casanova, Marie Bernadette Darang, Simon Hageman, Irina Dvorak, Rikard Liden, Nagaraja Harshadeep Rao, and Marcus Wishart. The team worked under the guidance of Benoit Bosquet and Magda Lovei (practice managers for Environment and Natural Resources in the Africa region) and under the general oversight of Francisco Ferreira, chief economist for the Africa Region of the World Bank.

In the World Bank's External and Corporate Relations, Publishing and Knowledge unit, Susan Graham managed the book production process and Abdia Mohamed handled acquisition duties.

The analysis is based on a consulting report prepared by a team comprised of Jennie Barron, Deveraj de Condappa, Stephanie Galaitsi, Brian Joyce, Annette Huber-Lee, David Purkey, and David Yates at the Stockholm Environment Institute (SEI); Nicholas Burger, David Groves, Robert Lempert, and Zhimin Mao at the RAND Corporation; Oliver Broad, Mark Howells, and Vignesh Sridharan at the Royal Institute of Technology–Sweden (KTH); Kenneth M. Strzepek of the Massachusetts Institute of Technology; and Brent Boehlert, Yohannes Gebretsadik,

James E. Neumann, and Lisa Rennels at Industrial Economics, Incorporated. The broader team also included other consultants and partners in Africa and in the United States, including Mohamed Elshamy, Ephrem Getahun, Mohamed Abdoulahi Hassan, Mohamed Ahmed Hassan, and Abdulkarim Seid at the Nile Basin Initiative; Casey Brown and Katherine Lownsbery from the University of Massachusetts; the International Institute for Water and the Environment; Denis Hughes, Sukhmani Mantel, and Raphael Tshimanga of Rhodes University; and Bruce Hewitson and Chris Jack from the University of Cape Town.

The World Bank Group peer reviewers were Julia Bucknall and Marianne Fay. Helpful comments were also provided by Luciano Canali, Jane Ebinger, Stephane Hallegatte, and Jamal Saghir. We also wish to acknowledge the helpful comments from Mekuria Beyene, adviser for Transboundary Water Management to the New Partnership for Africa's Development (NEPAD).

We wish to thank the participants in the stakeholder workshop in Maseru, Lesotho, in July 2013: Sonwabo Damba, Richard Dominique, B. T. Khatibe, Doctor Lukhele, F. Maladamola, Tatuker Maseltias, Nginani Mbayi, David Mbidi, N. Mokhabuli, Phooko Mokose, Rudolph Muttembo, Kaangu Nguasananonsombe, Peter Nthathakane, Obolokile Obakeng, Nic Oppermand, Rapule Pule, Luther Rakira, Drake Rukundo, Thato Setloboko, Tente Tente, Lenka Thamae, Theletame Theletame, M. Tlali, Fred Tuitomola, and Douglas Unachach. We also wish to thank the participants in the stakeholder workshop in Accra, Ghana, in October 2013: Tozo Agbedidi Abla, Agamah Komi Agbedumasi, Barnabas Amisigo, Ben Ampomah, Samuel Bem Ayangeaor, Nii Boi Ayibotele, Juati Ayilari-Naa, Robert Désiré T. Belibi, Albert Bere, Maxwell Boateng-Gyimah, Navon Cisse, Jean Abdias Compaore, Paul Compaore, Sebastien Konan Kouame, Jacques Kraidi, and Porgo Mahamadi. Finally, we wish to thank the participants to the Expert Group Meeting convened in Addis Ababa, Ethiopia, April 2–3, 2015, by the African Union Commission and UNECA. These include Ahiataku Wisdom Togobo, Mathilde Bord-Laurans, Stéphanie Leyronas, Edith B. Tibahwa, Bayaornibe Dabire, Dumsani Mndzebele, John Mungai, Mohammed El-Shamy, Henri-Claude Enoumba, Lenka Thamae, Evans Kaseke, Bob Mwangala, Johnson Maviya, Jean-Chrysostome Mekondongo, Laila Oulkacha, Maiga Amadou, Yohannes Gebretsadik, Wilfran Mofouma, Joseph Intsiful, Thierry Amoussougbo, Kidist Belayneh, and Charles Muraya.

Financial support from the following donors and trust funds is gratefully acknowledged: The U.K. Department for International Development (DfID); the Nordic Development Fund (NDF); the Kreditanstalt fur Entwicklung (KfW); the Agence Française de Développement (AFD); the Bank-Netherland Partnership Program (BNPP); and the Trust Fund for Environmentally and Socially Sustainable Development (TFESSD). The following staff were part of the donor's steering group for the study: Hannu Eerola and Aage Jorgensen (NDF); Nicola Jenns (DFID); Mathilde Bord-Laurans (AFD); and Ulf Moslener (representing KfW).

About the Contributors

Editors

Raffaello Cervigni is a lead environmental economist with the Africa Region of the World Bank. He holds an MA and a PhD in economics from Oxford University and University College London, and has 18 years of professional experience on programs, projects, and research in a variety of sectors financed by the World Bank, the GEF, the European Union, and the Italian government. He is currently the World Bank's regional coordinator for climate change in the Africa region, after serving for about three years in a similar role for the Middle East and North Africa region. He is the author or co-author of more than 40 technical papers and publications, including books, book chapters, and journal articles.

Rikard Liden has an MS in civil engineering and a PhD in water resources engineering from Lund University, Sweden. He specializes in the modeling of complex water systems and has authored numerous scientific research papers. He has more than 20 years of professional experience consulting for infrastructure development and management. He joined the World Bank in 2011 as a senior hydropower specialist, supporting the World Bank's projects on hydropower and dams globally.

James E. Neumann is principal and environmental economist at Industrial Economics, Incorporated, a Cambridge, Massachusetts, consulting firm that specializes in the economic analysis of environmental policies. Neumann is the editor of two World Bank books on adaptation to climate change in the agriculture sector; coeditor with Robert Mendelsohn of *The Impact of Climate Change on the United States Economy*, an integrated analysis of economic welfare impacts in multiple economic sectors, including energy, agriculture, and water resources; and author of multiple journal articles on climate change impacts and adaptation in the infrastructure sector, including in developing countries. He specializes in the economics of adaptation to climate change and is a lead author for the Intergovernmental Panel on Climate Change Working Group II chapter "Economics of Adaptation."

Kenneth M. Strzepek is a research scientist at MIT's Joint Program on the Science and Policy of Global Change; an adjunct lecturer of Public Policy at the Harvard Kennedy School of Government; a non-resident senior fellow at the United Nations University–World Institute for Development Economics Research; and a professor emeritus at the University of Colorado. Professor Strzepek has edited two books on climate change and water resources, and he has authored many journal articles on the nexus of environmental and economic systems for sustainable development. He was a lead author of the Fifth and Second Intergovernmental Panel on Climate Change (IPCC) Assessments. He was an Arthur Maass–Gilbert White Fellow at the Institute for Water Resources of the U.S. Army Corps of Engineers and received the U.S. Department of Interior Citizen's Award for Innovation in the applications of systems analysis to water management. He is a corecipient of the Zayed International Prize for the Environment, and as a lead author for IPCC, he is a corecipient of the 2007 Nobel Peace Prize.

Authors

Evan Bloom is a principal data scientist for Capital One Labs, where he uses big data and machine learning to inform personal financial decision making. Previously, while at the RAND Corporation, he specialized in planning under deeply uncertain conditions. He used computational experiments, analytics, and visualizations to support policy decision makers in water resources, energy, and public health. He has worked with the U.S. Bureau of Reclamation, the World Bank, the California Department of Water, the Los Angeles Department of Public Health, and several local water agencies. He recently completed his PhD dissertation on strategies that respond to new information, a tool to address water delivery reliability in the face of uncertain climate conditions in the western United States. He holds a BA in political science and a BS in management science from University of California, San Diego, and a PhD in policy analysis from the Pardee RAND Graduate School.

Brent Boehlert is a senior associate at Industrial Economics, Inc., with more than 10 years of experience consulting on water resource issues. He specializes in water resource engineering and economics, with a focus on climate change impact and adaptation analyses, river basin planning, and project design under uncertainty. He brings a specialized set of analytical tools to his often inter-disciplinary project work, and has applied those tools as the lead analyst on more than 20 projects in more than 10 countries. He has extensive experience analyzing the economic contribution of water resources to various economic sectors, including agriculture, hydropower, and municipal and industrial uses, and has done several such evaluations in Africa, Central Asia, Eastern Europe, and the United States. Dr. Boehlert holds a PhD in water resources engineering from Tufts University, an MS in natural resource economics from Oregon State University, and an AB in engineering from Dartmouth College.

Oliver Broad joined the Royal Institute of Technology's division of Energy Systems Analysis (KTH-dESA) in 2012. With a background in mechanical and energy engineering, his research uses various analytical platforms to develop optimization models in support of energy planning. He uses a cost minimization approach to scenario analysis and is involved in work that concentrates on the Africa region, assessing the national and power pool–level implications of various energy pathways. Previous and current projects include analyzing prospects for renewable energy in northern and eastern Africa with the International Renewable Energy Agency, participating in mapping rural electrification solutions for Nigeria and Ethiopia as a contribution to the International Energy Agency's *Africa Energy Outlook* (2014), and assessing the shift to sustainable energy and transportation systems in Uganda by 2050. His responsibilities at KTH-dESA also include course management and lecturing on optimization and systems analysis.

Casey Brown is associate professor in the Department of Civil and Environmental Engineering at the University of Massachusetts, Amherst. He has a PhD in environmental engineering Science from Harvard University and led the water team at the International Research Institute (IRI) for Climate and Society at Columbia University. His has worked extensively on projects around the world in this regard. He has received the Presidential Early Career Award for Science and Engineering, the National Science Foundation CAREER award, and the Huber Research Prize from the American Society of Civil Engineers. Dr. Brown's work is funded by the National Science Foundation, NOAA, Department of Defense, World Bank, and the U.S. Army Corps of Engineers. He is associate editor of the *ASCE Journal of Water Resources Planning and Management*, and he chairs the Water Resources Planning under Climate Change Technical Committee of the ASCE Environmental and Water Resources Institute Systems Committee and the Water and Society Technical Committee of the AGU Hydrology Section.

Fatima Denton is currently the coordinator of the African Climate Policy Centre and the director of the Special Initiatives Division, a natural resource management division of the United Nations Economic Commission for Africa, which she joined in 2012. Prior to 2012, she led one of the largest adaptation research programs for six years managing a portfolio of more than 45 projects on pro-poor adaptation across 33 countries in Africa. She joined IDRC in 2006 after working as a senior energy scientist with the United Nations Environment Program (UNEP) in Denmark, where she worked on energy poverty, climate adaptation, and policy matters relating to energy SMEs and institutional governance. She has written articles on energy poverty, gender and energy, and climate change adaptation. She is a coordinating lead author for the Working Group II Fifth Assessment of Intergovernmental

Panel on Climate Change (IPCC). She has had an eclectic academic background, and holds a PhD in political science and development studies from the University of Birmingham (UK).

Stephanie Galaitsi is a research scientist at the U.S. Center of the Stockholm Environment Institute. She holds a master's degree from Tufts University in environmental and water resources engineering and a bachelor's degree from Carleton College in Middle East history. Her study areas include domestic water demand, water modeling systems, and water insecurity.

Yohannes Gebretsadik is a water resource engineering and modeling expert who has participated in large-scale water resource engineering projects since 2003. His focus is mainly within the Nile basin, in the areas of flood protection and early warning, transboundary joint multipurpose projects, irrigation and drainage, watershed management, basin-wide hydrologic studies, and development of planning and decision support tools. His role in this work focused on development and application of the perfect foresight basin-scale optimization tool. Dr. Gebretsadik holds a PhD in water resources engineering from the University of Colorado at Boulder. He also holds an MS in hydraulic engineering and a BS in civil engineering from Addis Ababa University.

David Groves is a senior policy researcher at the RAND Corporation, a co-director of the RAND Water and Climate Resilience Center, and a core faculty member at the Pardee RAND Graduate School. He specializes in improving the long-term planning and decision making of natural resource planning agencies through the application of innovative analytics and decision support tools. He works with planners in the water resources, energy, and coastal sectors. He has worked with the World Bank; several state governments, including California and Louisiana; and many water agencies across the United States to develop climate adaptation plans. Dr. Groves earned a BS in geological and environmental science and an MS in earth systems from Stanford University. He earned an MS in atmospheric sciences from the University of Washington, and a PhD in policy analysis from the Pardee RAND Graduate School.

Bruce Hewitson is the South Africa National Research chair on climate change and director of the Climate System Analysis Group (CSAG) at the University of Cape Town (UCT). He completed his undergraduate degrees at the University of Cape Town, followed by a MS and PhD from Pennsylvania State University. His expertise and research focuses include regional climate change, climate modeling, downscaling, the interface of climate science and society, and capacity building on climate change. Bruce currently co-chairs the World Climate Research Program's (WCRP) Working Group on Regional Climate as well as the IPCC Task Force on data in support of climate impact and analysis. He was a coordinating lead author in the IPCC's Third, Fourth, and Fifth Assessment Reports.

He leads a wide range of projects spanning urban decision making under climate change, climate change projections, seasonal forecasting, uncertainty, and analytical methods.

Mark Howells directs the division and holds the chair of Energy Systems Analysis at the Royal Institute of Technology (KTH-dESA) in Sweden. He has an honorary professorship at the University of Technology in Sydney. He leads the development of the world's premier open source energy planning software, has published in nature journals, coordinates the European Commission's think tank for energy (INSIGHT_E), and is regularly used by the United Nations as a policy-science expert. His division in Sweden undertakes research for the National Aeronautics and Space Administration (NASA), International Renewable Energy Agency (IRENA), the World Bank, and others. Prior to joining KTH-dESA, he had an award-winning career with the International Atomic Energy Agency. As a student, he was the spokesperson for the World Energy Council youth program of 1998.

Annette Huber-Lee leads the Water-Food-Energy Nexus for the Stockholm Environment Institute (SEI). In addition, she is a senior scientist, focusing on water resource management, economics, and policy. She returned to the U.S. Center of the Stockholm Environment Institute after serving as director of SEI Asia, in Bangkok, from mid-2012 until February 2013. She has more than 20 years of professional experience in international and domestic planning and management of environmental and water resources. She focuses on the integration of economic, engineering, and ecological approaches to solve environmental and social problems in a comprehensive and sustainable manner, and on the development of innovative approaches to environmental policy and natural resource conflict management. She has a PhD in engineering sciences from Harvard University, an MS in civil engineering from the Massachusetts Institute of Technology, and a BS in agricultural engineering from Cornell University.

Denis Hughes has more than 35 years experience in the development and application of hydrological and water resource estimation models. He received a PhD from University College of Wales, Aberystwyth, in 1976. He has been affiliated with Rhodes University as associate professor, 1984–88, and professor, 1988–2002; and he has been the director of the Institute for Water Research (IWR) from 2003 until the present. His current activities include the development of improved parameter estimation methods for conceptual hydrologic models, which are widely applied in southern Africa, and projects associated with the application of models in the Okavango Basin in southwestern Africa, South Africa, and the Dominican Republic. Over the past 10 years, he has been involved in the development and application of methods to support the determination and implementation of environmental flow requirements, especially for ephemeral rivers, and in activities associated with the implementation of water use licensing and real-time management of resources.

Chris Jack is a researcher in the Climate Systems Analysis Group at the University of Cape Town, South Africa. As part of his mission to meet the knowledge needs of responding climate variability and change, Mr. Jack incorporates high performance computing and big data into decision-making theory and social engagement. His publications examine climate processes in the southern Africa region to inform decision making and development.

Brian Joyce is a senior scientist in the Water and Sanitation unit at the Stockholm Environment Institute (SEI). He has a PhD in hydrologic sciences from the University of California, Davis, and more than 15 years of experience in planning and management of water resources in the American West and in the international arena. His research at SEI focuses on the development of decision support tools for water resource systems and he has participated in the development and application of databases and tools used for water resource analysis in a variety of settings worldwide. His recent work has included using SEI's Water Evaluation and Planning (WEAP) model to assess climate change impacts on agriculture, to design optimal approaches for meeting environmental flow requirements, and to create an analytical platform for use in multiparty discussions of transboundary water resource issues.

Robert Lempert is a senior scientist at the RAND Corporation and director of the Frederick S. Pardee Center for Longer Range Global Policy and the Future Human Condition. His research focuses on risk management and decision making under conditions of deep uncertainty, with an emphasis on climate change, energy, and the environment. Dr. Lempert is a fellow of the American Physical Society, a member of the Council on Foreign Relations, a lead author for Working Group II of the United Nations' Intergovernmental Panel on Climate Change (IPCC) Fifth Assessment Report, and a lead author of the U.S. National Climate Assessment. Dr. Lempert was the Inaugural EADS Distinguished Visitor in Energy and Environment at the American Academy in Berlin. A professor of policy analysis in the Pardee RAND Graduate School, Dr. Lempert is an author of the book *Shaping the Next One Hundred Years: New Methods for Quantitative, Longer-Term Policy Analysis.*

Zhimin Mao is a doctoral fellow at the Pardee RAND Graduate School and an assistant policy analyst at the RAND Corporation. Her research interests include energy, environmental policy, and economic development. Combining academic and work experiences, she participated in the Global Governance 2022 program and co-authored a report analyzing global energy governance scenarios in the next decade. Her experiences prior to RAND focused on energy and environmental policy. During her time at the Heinz Center for Science,

Economics and Environment, and at the University Corporation for Atmospheric Research, she worked on issues related to U.S. and Chinese collaboration on low-carbon development. She was an international consultant and summer intern at the Asian Development Bank, where she conducted a household energy usage survey and completed a project aimed at developing affordable energy efficiency solutions for extremely poor families. Her undergraduate honors thesis on supply chain strength and sustainable development was published by the *Journal of Cleaner Production*.

David Purkey leads the Water Group at the Stockholm Environment Institute's (SEI) U.S. Center. Much of his work centers on the development, dissemination, and application of SEI's Water Evaluation and Planning (WEAP) system. His research interests include understanding the potential impacts of and adaptation to climate change in the water sector and aquatic ecosystems, integrated water resource management that focuses on linking the management of surface water and groundwater to meet a broad spectrum of objectives, and equitable management of transboundary water resources and the use of models within broadly subscribed participatory water planning exercises. Purkey and his team are experienced in applying a range of hydrologic, hydraulic, and planning models in settings as diverse as California, the Andes, the U.S.-Mexico border, and West and Southern Africa. He received his PhD in hydrology from the University of California, Davis, in 1998.

Abdulkarim Seid has more than two decades of experience in academia, research, policy analysis, and consulting in the water sector. He is currently the head of Nile Basin Initiative (NBI)–Water Resources Management Department, the technical arm of the NBI, which has core mandates of policy analyses and formulations, analytic work, knowledge management, river basin monitoring, and capacity building. Dr. Seid obtained his PhD from University of Technology, Darmstadt (Germany). He has been an assistant professor at Addis Ababa University. Dr. Seid led the development and operationalization of the Nile Basin Decision Support System (DSS), a comprehensive analytic framework for water resources planning and management. He is in charge of the operationalization of the Nile Basin Sustainability Framework, which is a suite of policies, strategies, and guidelines required to inform sustainable water resources management and development in the Nile basin. He is currently leading the basin-wide analytic work in the Nile basin using a set of modeling and analytic tools for addressing strategic water resources issues.

Vignesh Sridharan has worked as a researcher at the Royal Institute of Technology's Unit of Energy Systems Analysis (KTH-dESA) in Sweden since October 2012. His work focuses on the development of OSeMOSYS, the Open Source Energy Modeling System. Currently, he is involved in a project with the United Nations Department of Economic and Social Affairs to link energy system models and computable general equilibrium models, for which he interacts closely with the energy ministries of Bolivia, Nicaragua, and Uganda. Recently, he finished a project funded by the World Bank to assess the impact of climate change on African energy infrastructure, during which he developed energy systems models for African power pools. He holds a dual MSc in energy systems engineering from KTH and the Polytechnic University of Catalonia, Barcelona. Prior to working on his masters degree, he worked as a research and development engineer at Robert Bosch GmbH for two years.

Mehmet Ümit Taner is an environmental engineer and a PhD candidate at the University of Massachusetts, Amherst. He specializes in environmental modeling and decision making under uncertainty. Over the past 10 years, he has been involved in multidisciplinary projects on integrated watershed planning, ecological modeling, and wastewater treatment. Previously he had worked at the Scientific and Technological Research Council of Turkey (TUBITAK-MRC) as a researcher, and at the U.S. Environmental Protection Agency (EPA) Office of Water, as an Oak Ridge Institute for Science and Education (ORISE) fellow. Currently his work focuses on water infrastructure planning under deep climate and socioeconomic uncertainty. He is particularly interested in the integration of vulnerability-based planning approaches and robust optimization for ensuring long-term water, food, and energy security. His current work focuses on Africa, in particular Kenya, Malawi, and the Niger River basin.

Abbreviations

ACPC	African Climate Policy Centre
AFD	Agence Française de Développement
AICD	Africa Infrastructure Country Diagnostic
AR4	IPCC Fourth Assessment Report
AR5	IPCC Fifth Assessment Report
BCSD	Bias Corrected Spatial Disaggregation
BNPP	Bank-Netherland Partnership Program
CMI	Climate Moisture Index
CMIP	Coupled Model Intercomparison Project
CO_2	carbon dioxide
DFID	U.K. Department for International Development
EAC	East African Community
EAPP	Eastern Africa Power Pool
ESRI	Environmental Systems Research Institute
FAO	Food and Agriculture Organization of the United Nations
GCM	general circulation model
GHCN	Global Historical Climatology Network
GIS	geographic information system
GW	gigawatt
Ha	hectare
ICA	Infrastructure Consortium for Africa
ICOLD	International Commission on Large Dams
IFPRI	International Food Policy Research Institute
IMPACT	International Model for Policy Analysis of Agricultural Commodities and Trade
IPCC	Intergovernmental Panel on Climate Change

IRENA	International Renewable Energy Agency
ITRC	Irrigation Training and Research Center
IWMI	International Water Management Institute
KfW	Kreditanstalt fur Entwicklung
LHWP	Lesotho Highlands Water Project
MSIOA	Multi-Sector Investment Opportunities Analysis
NBA	Niger Basin Authority
NDF	Nordic Development Fund
NGO	nongovernmental organization
NPV	net present value
O&M	operation and maintenance
OSeMOSYS	Open Source Energy Modeling System
PAP	Priority Action Plan
PF	perfect foresight
PIDA	Programme for Infrastructure Development in Africa
PPA	Power Purchase Agreement
PV	present value
RCC	roller-compacted concrete
RCP	representative concentration pathway
RDM	robust decision making
SADC	Southern African Development Community
SAPP	Southern African Power Pool
SDAP	Sustainable Development Action Plan
SEI	Stockholm Environment Institute
TDH	Turn Down the Heat
TFESSD	Trust Fund for Environmentally and Socially Sustainable Development
THI	Temperature Humidity Index
TOR	terms of reference
TWh	terawatt hour
UNFCCC	United Nations Framework Convention on Climate Change
WAPP	West African Power Pool
WEAP	Water Evaluation and Planning
WHO	World Health Organization
WMO	World Meteorological Organization

Key Messages

To sustain Africa's growth and accelerate the eradication of extreme poverty, investment in infrastructure is fundamental. In 2010, the Africa Infrastructure Country Diagnostic found that to enable Africa to fill its infrastructure gap, some US\$93 billion per year for the next decade will need to be invested. The Program for Infrastructure Development in Africa (PIDA), endorsed in 2012 by the continent's heads of state and government, lays out an ambitious long-term plan for closing Africa's infrastructure gap, including trough major increases in hydroelectric power generation and water storage capacity. Much of this investment will support the construction of long-lived infrastructure (for example, dams, power stations, and irrigation canals), which may be vulnerable to changes in climatic patterns—yet the direction and magnitude of these climatic changes remain significantly uncertain.

This book evaluates—using for the first time a single consistent methodology* and a wide range of state-of-the-art future climate scenarios—the impacts of climate change on hydropower and irrigation expansion plans in Africa's main river basins (Congo, Niger, Nile, Orange, Senegal, Volta, and Zambezi), as well as the effects on the electricity sector across four power pools (West, Eastern, Central, and Southern power pools).

The book demonstrates that failure to integrate climate change in the planning and design of power and water infrastructure could entail, in the driest scenarios, significant losses of hydropower revenues and increases in consumer expenditure for energy. In the wettest climate scenarios, business-as-usual infrastructure development could lead to substantial forgone revenues if the larger volume of precipitation is not used to expand the production of hydropower. Within the limits of methods used and the data available to the study

---

* In addition to the summary discussion contained in this book, the methodology of analysis is described in detail in technical appendixes accessible online at https://openknowledge.worldbank.org/handle/10986/21875.

team, it is estimated that the dry scenario loss of hydropower revenue would range between 5 percent and 60 percent of the no-climate-change baseline (depending on the basin), with increases in consumer expenditure for energy up to three times the corresponding baseline values, as a result of dwindling production of hydropower. The potential forgone revenue in the wettest climate scenario is estimated to be the in the range of 15–130 percent of the baseline. In irrigation, the largest loss in revenue is in the range of 10–20 percent for most basins. In wet scenarios, the largest forgone gains are estimated to be in the range of 1–4 percent, with the exception of the Volta basin, where they are projected to be one order of magnitude higher.

The main message of this book is that proper integration of climate change in the planning and design of infrastructure investments supported by PIDA, regional, and national plans can reduce considerably the risk posed by the climate of the future to the physical and economic performance of hydropower and irrigation investments. But African countries do not need to slow the pace of infrastructure investment. As long as climate risk analysis is fully integrated in the project cycle, starting from the upstream planning stages at the national, river basin, regional, and power-pool levels, and in pre-feasibility studies of individual investments, climate risks can be significantly mitigated in a cost-effective manner.

Proper integration of climate change in infrastructure investment needs to properly address the challenge posed by the large and persistent uncertainty surrounding climate projections. If it were known in advance that a wet future would materialize, it would make sense to expand generation capacity to produce more hydropower; in a dry future, it is preferable to reduce generation capacity to avoid sinking capital in equipment that will end up being underutilized. But the climate of the future is not known in advance. While ignoring climate change entails serious risks of planning and designing infrastructure that is not suited for the climate of the future, there is also a risk of adapting to climate change in the wrong way, which could be as significant as the risk of incurring damages when not adapting. A wrong adaptation decision takes place, for example, when it is based on the expectation that the future will be drier, when in fact, it turns out to be wetter.

The solution to this dilemma is to identify an adaptation strategy that balances the risk of inaction with the risk of wrong action, taking into account the preferences of decision makers and attitudes toward risks. The illustrative assessment conducted in this book through a desk-based analysis suggests that in the case of hydropower, this approach to adaptation under climate uncertainty can cut in half (or more) the maximum climate change impact (loss of revenue or missed opportunity to increase it) that would be faced in the case of inaction. The analysis further suggests that the benefits in terms of reduced risks significantly exceed the cost of modifying baseline investment plans in all basins, with the exception of the Congo basin, where climate projections concur in pointing to limited expected changes in the current hydrological regime, making the economic case for modifying existing plans less compelling.

The specific way in which infrastructure planning and design should be modified, however, depends crucially on attitudes toward risks, time preferences, and the relative priority assigned to the physical performance versus the economic performance of infrastructure—within and across sectors. These are choices that countries and regional organizations will need to make themselves; the results presented in this book are therefore indicative and should not be intended as a substitute for assessments reflecting the full range of stakeholder's information, perspectives, and priorities.

Promoting adaptation to climate change in the planning and design of infrastructure is likely to require a change in mindset, away from consolidated behavior and practices, with the goal of better integrating the expertise of the relevant professions, such as climate scientists and design engineers. Because such a paradigm shift is likely to have a considerable gestation time, the time to act is now, with priority assigned to the following selected areas of interventions.

1. **Develop technical guidelines on the integration of climate change in the planning and design of infrastructure in climate-sensitive sectors.** A multi-stakeholder technical working group could be established to develop voluntary technical guidelines on how to apply the notions of climate resilience, discussed at length in this book, to real-life infrastructure planning and design.

2. **Promote an open-data knowledge repository for climate-resilient infrastructure development.** To bring down the cost of the analysis needed to integrate climate considerations into infrastructure development, there is a need to establish common data sources (on climate scenarios, hydrology, standard construction costs, etc.), which could be made available to the public on open-data platforms and hosted by African institutions (such as the African Climate Policy Center of the United Nations Economic Commission for Africa).

3. **Establish an Africa climate resilience project preparation facility.** The facility, which would be adequately financed with grant or concessional resources, could have different windows to cater to the specific needs of different sectors or for different stages of the infrastructure development cycle. For example, the facility could provide support to climate-resilient infrastructure master plans or to the integration of climate resilience into individual projects.

4. **Launch training programs for climate-resilient infrastructure professionals.** To ensure adequate strengthening of the technical skills that

are required to enhance the climate resilience of infrastructure, one or more training programs could be established for professionals involved in the planning, design, and operation of climate-sensitive infrastructures.

5. **Set up an observatory on climate-resilient infrastructure development in Africa.** To ensure that the work at the technical level (discussed above on methodology, data, and project preparation) and training retains visibility and linkages with the policy level of decision making, an observatory on climate-resilient infrastructure development could be established.

Overview

*Raffaello Cervigni, James E. Neumann, Rikard Liden,
Kenneth M. Strzepek*

Africa's Infrastructure: A Key to Development but Potentially Vulnerable to Climate Change

Africa has experienced economic growth of more than 5 percent per annum during the past decade, but to sustain this growth, investment in infrastructure is fundamental. In recognition of this fact, the Program for Infrastructure Development in Africa (PIDA), endorsed in 2012 by the continent's heads of state and government, has laid out an ambitious, long-term plan for closing Africa's infrastructure gap. In the water and power sector, PIDA calls for an expansion of hydroelectric power generation capacity by more than 54,000 megawatts (MW) and of water storage capacity by 20,000 cubic kilometers.

Much of these investments will support the construction of long-lived infrastructure (e.g., dams, power stations, and irrigation canals), which will be vulnerable to the potentially harsher climate of the future. This book is the first to use a consistent approach across river basins and power systems in Africa, including a comprehensive, broad set of state-of-the-art climate projections to evaluate the risks posed by climate change to planned investments in Africa's water and power sectors. It further analyzes how investment plans could be modified to mitigate those risks, and it quantifies the corresponding benefits and costs, within the limits of a largely desk-based assessment.

The scope of the study includes seven major river basins (Congo, Niger, Nile, Senegal, Upper Orange, Volta, and Zambezi) and four power pools (Central, Eastern, Southern, and West). The study addresses all the PIDA hydropower capacity enhancements in the subject basins, as part of the region's overall power generation plans, as well as additional investments in irrigation that are included in regional and national master plans.

The reference investment program against which climate effects are assessed (labeled as PIDA+ in this book, to cover national master plans not included in PIDA proper) calls for a major scale-up of the stock of infrastructure capacity across the continent's major river basins (figure O.1). Hydropower capacity is planned to increase by a factor of six, and the irrigated area by 60 percent—but up to 700 percent in some basins. The total present value of the investment

Figure O.1 **Planned Expansion of Hydropower and Irrigation Capacity**
(2010 capacity = 1)

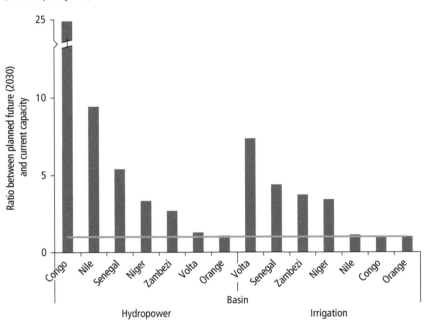

Note: Congo hydropower expansion includes a portion of the Grand Inga phased hydropower project, which is expected to be constructed by 2050, but is currently not expected to be fully operational until after 2050. The green line represents a ratio of one, equivalent to current capacity.

cost to achieve these goals is estimated at $75 billion over the period 2015–50. The window of opportunity for making investment more climate resilient is considerable. We estimate that of the roughly 80,000 megawatts (MW) of future additional hydropower capacity envisioned in PIDA+, only approximately 10 percent (or 8,500 MW) is in facilities already under construction. Most of the existing construction activity is accounted for by one large project, the 6,000 MW Grand Ethiopian Renaissance Dam.

This massive program of investment is, by and large, being designed on the basis of the historical climate. But a vast body of scientific evidence indicates that the climate of the future will be very different from that of the past, although climate models often disagree on whether the future in any specific location will be drier or wetter (figure O.2). In addition, the range of uncertainty in climate projections has tended to increase over time—the earlier-generation climate model results, in blue in figure O.2, show a tighter distribution than the latest

Figure O.2 Climate Change Projections across Africa's River Basins

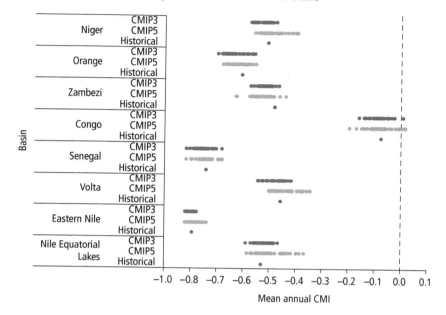

Note: The Climate Moisture Index (CMI) is a measure of aridity that combines the effect of rainfall and temperature projections. For example, higher temperatures would increase evaporation. The index values vary between −1 and +1, with lower values representing more arid conditions. A CMI value greater than zero indicates that, for that basin, precipitation rates are greater than potential evapotranspiration rates. CMI is often a good proxy indicator for measures such as river runoff and irrigation demands. The chart reports CMI values (averaged over the period 2010–50) projected by climate models included in the Intergovernmental Panel on Climate Change (IPCC) Fourth and Fifth Assessment Reports. In each basin, the red dot denotes the average value of CMI in the historical baseline. Dots to the right of the historical value refer to projections of wetter climate; dots to the left indicate projections of drier climate. CMIP3 corresponds to the IPCC Fourth Assessment General Circulation Model (GCM) results (published in 2007); CMIP5 corresponds to the IPCC Fifth Assessment GCM results (published in 2013).

climate model results, shown in green. The most recent advances in climate science, therefore, do not help narrow uncertainty, which on the contrary seems to be increasing. This conclusion provides another important rationale for adopting the robust decision-making methods used in this study when planning climate-sensitive infrastructure deployment.

Risk of Inaction

Climate change will bring about major variations in Africa's hydrological regimes. The total amount of annual rainfall, its monthly distribution over the year, and the way it will evaporate or contribute to runoff will all be quite different from the past. As a result, the amount of water available to key productive uses, such as hydropower or irrigation, will be very different: lower in dry climate scenarios, higher in wet scenarios. These changes will affect considerably the performance of infrastructure in physical terms. Climate change is likely to result in significant deviations from the amount of hydropower or irrigated crops that would be produced under a stationary climate. For example, in the case of the Central and Southern Africa basins (Congo, Orange, and Zambezi), depending on the climate scenario considered, there could be underperformance in the power and water sectors, occurring in many scenarios; overperformance by both sectors, occurring in some scenarios; and, in fewer cases, underperformance by one sector and overperformance by the other (figure O.3).

In economic terms, the impacts of climate change include lost revenues from underperforming hydropower or irrigation infrastructure in drier climate

Figure O.3 Changes in Physical Performance of Hydropower and Irrigation under Climate Change in the Congo, Orange, and Zambezi Basins, 2015–50

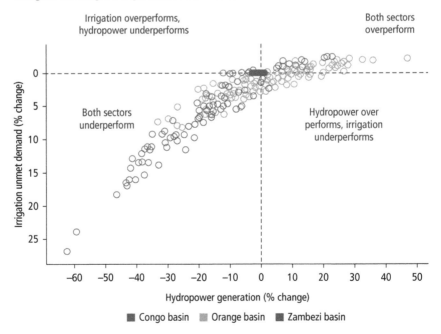

Note: Each circle represents a particular climate scenario. Figures are expressed as percentage differences from the value that would be expected under no climate change. Historical performance is approximated by the intersection of the two dashed reference lines (at 0 percent change).

futures and, by contrast, the opportunity cost of not taking advantage of an abundance of exploitable water resources in wetter climate futures.

In simulations of the economic performance of infrastructure in the climate scenario at the end of the range, the deviations from the results expected under a historical climate are dramatic. In hydropower (figure O.4), dry scenarios lead to revenue losses on the order of 10–60 percent of baseline values, with the Nile (Equatorial Lakes region), Senegal, and Zambezi basins most affected. Wet scenarios result in potential revenue increases on the order of 20–140 percent (with the Eastern Nile, Niger, and Volta basins having the largest gains).

In some wetter climate futures, infrastructure could perform better than expected, because for a given installed capacity, more hydropower or more crops could be produced with the extra water. However, many of the corresponding gains could be only potential ones, because power systems would have

Figure O.4 Changes in Hydropower Revenues from Climate Change, 2015–50
(Present value)

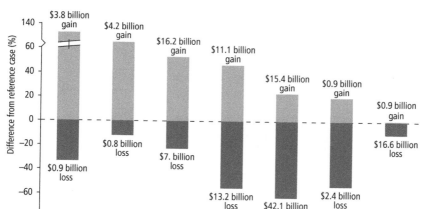

Note: The bars reflect, for each basin, the range of economic outcomes across all climate futures; that is, the highest increase (green bars) and highest decrease (red bars) of hydropower revenues (discounted at 3 percent), relative to the no-climate-change reference case. The outlier bar corresponding to the Volta basin has been trimmed to avoid distorting the scale of the chart and skewing the values for the other basins. Estimates reflect the range, but not the distribution, of economic outcomes across all climate futures. Each basin's results reflect the best and worst scenarios for that basin alone, rather than the best and worst scenarios across all basins. The Orange basin is excluded because this study includes only the Upper Orange, where impacts are small relative to other basins.

Figure O.5 Changes in Irrigation Revenues from Climate Change, 2015–50
(Present value)

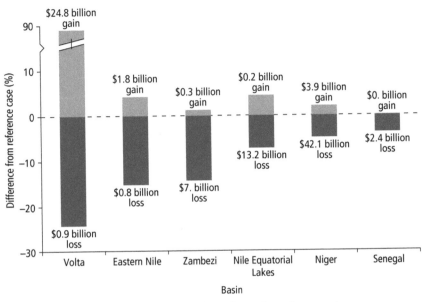

Note: The bars reflect, for each basin, the range of economic outcomes across all climate futures; that is, the highest increase (green bars) and highest decrease (red bars) of irrigation revenues (discounted at 3 percent), relative to the no-climate-change reference case. The outlier bar corresponding to the Volta basin has been trimmed to avoid distorting the scale of the chart and skewing the values for the other basins. Estimates reflect the range, but not the distribution, of economic outcomes across all climate futures. Each basin's results reflect the best and worst scenarios for that basin alone, rather than the best and worst scenarios across all basins. The Congo and Orange basins are excluded because the effects on irrigation are minimal.

been planned in anticipation of lower-than-actual generation from hydropower. As a result, the transmission lines and power trading agreements needed to bring the extra hydropower to the market may simply not be available; without them, the gains from more abundant water might not be realized.

In irrigation, departures from the no-climate-change baseline are also significant, but less striking (figure O.5). In dry scenarios, the largest loss in revenue is in the 5–20 percent range for most basins, corresponding to between $1 billion and $40 billion in absolute terms. In wet scenarios, the largest gains are in the Volta basin (more than 90 percent), but they are only in the range of 1–4 percent in the other basins. The figures in absolute terms are still notable, as the cases of the Eastern Nile and the Niger basins indicate (close to $2 billion and $4 billion in present value terms, respectively).

Since most of the effects of climate change will materialize in the outer decades of the simulation period, the magnitude of impacts will depend on how much decision makers care about the future. For example, using (as in most of this study) a 3 percent discount rate—which represents a considerable concern for how climate change might affect future well-being—the present value of hydropower and irrigation revenues expected in the Southern African Power Pool (SAPP) basins (Congo, Orange, and Zambezi) is on the order of $250 billion. But with a zero discount rate (no preference for the present over the future), this figure more than doubles, and so does the cost of losing revenues (in dry scenarios) or forgoing potential additional revenues (in wet scenarios). Conversely, when decision makers care more about the present (higher discount rates), the climate change impacts decrease. For example, when using a 7 percent discount rate, the present value of baseline revenues in the SAPP basins decrease by 60 percent.

In addition to affecting producer revenues, climate change can also have significant impacts on consumers. In wet climate futures, hydroelectric facilities generate larger amounts of electric power without any additional investment (more water spinning the same turbines faster), which in turn allows hydro to replace fossil fuel–based energy generation and reduces overall prices. But in dry climates, less hydropower than planned is produced, and the difference will need to be balanced by more expensive power sources, such as diesel generators. The results of the modeling simulations (figure O.6) for the Eastern Africa Power Pool (EAPP), SAPP, and West African Power Pool (WAPP) suggest that, in general, the effects are asymmetric, with the price increases in dry scenarios dominating the price decreases occurring in wet scenarios.

The effects on individual countries tend to be much greater than the power pool average. The dry scenario expenditure in Burundi, Malawi, and Sierra Leone is estimated to be two, three, and one and one-half times larger, respectively, than the no-climate-change baseline. Other vulnerable countries include, in Eastern Africa, Ethiopia, with a 40 percent increase, and in West Africa, Guinea and Mali, which are in the 40–60 percent range of increase. In countries with large fossil "backstop" options—such as South Africa and Nigeria—the expenditure increase under the dry climate scenario is less noticeable. Climate change has a greater effect on consumer prices in SAPP than in other power pools, owing to two factors: transmission limitations and the relatively high percentage of hydropower in most parts of SAPP (outside South Africa).

In addition to affecting expenditure on electricity, climate change can also have significant effects on expenditure for agricultural imports. In dry scenarios, irrigation underperforms compared with the no-climate-change scenario, and countries will need to make up for the deficit in food production

Figure O.6 Change in Cumulative Consumer Expenditure on Electricity Relative to the Reference Case

(No-climate-change case = 100%)

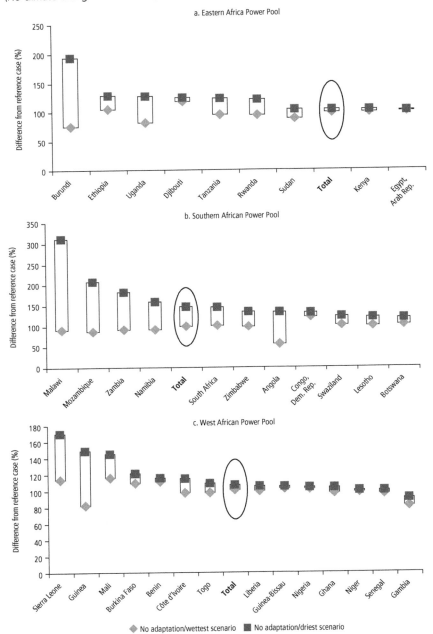

a. Eastern Africa Power Pool

b. Southern African Power Pool

c. West African Power Pool

◆ No adaptation/wettest scenario   ■ No adaptation/driest scenario

Note: The chart presents the change in cumulative consumer expenditure on power over the simulation period 2015–50, relative to the no-climate-change reference case and assuming no adaptation. Red squares represent expenditure change under the driest climate change scenario; green diamonds represent change under the wettest one.

Figure O.7 Cumulative Expenditure on Agricultural Imports
(No-climate-change case = 100)

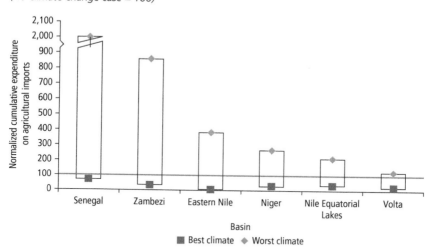

Note: The chart presents the change in cumulative (2015–50) expenditure on crop imports, relative to the no-climate-change reference case, for the driest and wettest climate change scenarios. Values greater than 100 indicate an increase in expenditure on imports caused by the lower production that would result under a drier climate; values less than 100 indicate an increase in domestic production, leading to a reduced need for imports. The outlier bar corresponding to the Volta basin has been trimmed to avoid distorting the scale of the chart and skewing the values for the other basins. Expenditures on imports are calculated with reference to the historical climate case. Imports are estimated as the additional need, or reduced need, to replace domestic irrigated agricultural production that is affected by climate change. Estimates are for cumulative import requirements through 2050. The Congo and Orange basins are excluded because the effects on irrigation and imports are minimal.

by increasing expenditure on crop imports. In the driest scenario, imports could be 1.5–20 times greater than the baseline, depending on the basin (figure O.7).

Adaptation to Climate Change under Uncertainty

To estimate the potential for adapting infrastructure capacity either to reduce damages or to take better advantage of favorable climatic conditions, the study estimates the optimal response for each of six representative climate futures, chosen to span the full range of climate futures across the seven basins considered. The adaptation strategies consist of combinations of basin- and farm-level design decisions (such as the size of reservoirs, turbine generation capacity, and the level of water-use efficiency at the basin and field levels). The resulting six adaptation strategies are equivalent to an optimal response to the corresponding climate future, which, as a first approximation, is assumed to be known in advance.

For example, knowing in advance that a wet future will materialize, it makes sense to expand generation capacity to produce more hydropower; in a dry future, it is preferable to reduce generation capacity to avoid sinking capital in equipment that will end up being underutilized. In this hypothetical "perfect foresight" situation, there is a wide scope for improving the performance of infrastructure. In the case of hydropower (figure O.8), dry scenario losses can be reduced by amounts equivalent to 5–40 percent of no-climate-change revenues; in wet scenarios, additional revenues can be generated, on the order of 5–60 percent of baseline revenues.

Obviously, the climate of the future *is not known in advance*. While ignoring climate change entails serious risks of planning and designing infrastructure that is not suited for the climate of the future, there is also a risk of adapting to climate change *in the wrong way*, which could be as significant as the risk of

Figure O.8 Gains from Perfect Foresight Adaptation in Hydropower

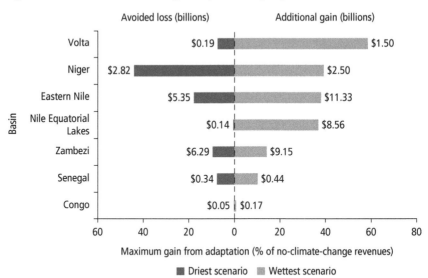

Note: Avoided losses (red bars) refer to the economic benefit of modifying investment decisions in anticipation of dry future climates. For example, reducing investments in turbines that would end up being underutilized would lead to cost savings. Additional gains (green bars) represent the gains that would accrue if planners correctly forecasted a future wetter climate and invested, for example, in expanded generation capacity to seize the opportunity of increasing hydropower production. The results for the Congo basin exclude changes to the Inga III and Grand Inga projects, which are held fixed in this analysis. The Orange basin is excluded from the adaptation analyses because the Upper Orange geographic study area includes no significant PIDA projects.

incurring damages when not adapting. A wrong adaptation decision takes place, for example, when it is based on the expectation that the future will be drier, when in fact, it turns out to be wetter.

Each of the six optimal adaptation strategies identified in response to a particular climate future carries the risk of generating damages (or "regrets") when a different climate materializes. In the Zambezi basin, for example, planners can ignore climate change when planning hydropower and later regret that decision, because it can generate a loss of about 18 percent of baseline revenues; but if they adapt in the wrong way, they can face a regret of close to 30 percent of baseline revenues (figure O.9).

The solution to this dilemma is to identify an adaptation strategy that balances the risk of inaction with the risk of wrong action, taking into account different possible preferences of decision makers and attitudes toward risks. One such preference is to avoid the worst outcome. In this case, the robust adaptation strategy is to minimize, over all possible future climates, the maximum regret (where "regrets" are the damages—loss of revenue or missed opportunity to increase it—caused by not selecting the best response to a particular climate). In addition to the mini-max criterion, the study also considers

Figure O.9 Damage from Not Adapting or Misadapting Hydropower Expansion Plans

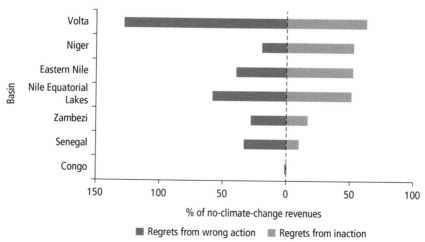

Note: The orange bars (regrets from inaction) indicate the greatest damage (expressed as a percentage of the no-climate-change revenues) that would be accrued when failing to consider climate change in investment planning. The damage could be a loss of revenues (in dry climates) or a forgone increase in revenues (in wet climates). The blue bars (regrets from wrong action) refer to the damage incurred when a particular climate change is anticipated (e.g., a drier climate) and a very different one actually unfolds (e.g., a wetter one). The Orange basin is excluded from the adaptation analyses because the Upper Orange geographic study area includes no significant PIDA projects.

alternative criteria (box O.1) for robust adaptations, which all suggest similar policy responses.

In the case of hydropower, such robust adaptation cuts in half, or more, the initial regrets—that is, those that would be faced in the case of inaction against climate change (figure O.10) in all basins, except in the case of the Congo basin, where initial regrets are small owing to an abundance of water.

BOX O.1

Criteria Used for Robust Adaptation

Mini-max regret, the main criterion used in this study, is not the only one that can be adopted for choosing robust adaptation strategies. When decision makers are uncertain about the future, the mini-max regret criterion suggests calculating the worst-case regret for each strategy over the full range of climate futures, and choosing the strategy with the smallest worst-case regret. The selection of the mini-max criterion is justifiable when decision makers do not have a way to assess the relative likelihood of different outcomes, and have high level of risk aversion. But in situations where there are reasons to believe that some outcomes are more likely than others and where policy makers are risk neutral, other decision criteria could be used (e.g., the expected utility criterion) that might lead to fairly different results.

To evaluate the sensitivity of the results of this study to alternative decision criteria, we considered three alternatives: mini-max regret, a criterion that selects the strategy with the smallest 90th percentile regret, and a criterion that selects the strategy with the smallest 75th percentile regret. In five of the six basins, all three criteria suggested the same robust adaptation strategy. In one basin (Zambezi), there was a small difference between the strategies selected by the mini-max regret and the 75th percentile criterion.

In the case of the project-level analysis, however, we considered three slightly more refined robustness criteria: mini-max regret, a criterion that selects the strategy with "small regrets" (that is, not exceeding a certain threshold) over the largest number of futures, and a criterion that selects the strategy with small expected regret for a wide range of likelihoods. For most of the five projects considered, the three criteria suggest similar robust adaptations, but not in all cases. For example, in the Lower Fufu project in Malawi (see map O.1), the mini-max regret criterion would lead to selecting the smallest diversion tunnel (with a maximum flow of 29 cubic meters per second [m³/s]). But the other two criteria would lead to larger sizes. The interpretation is that decision makers most concerned about very low flow/worst-case scenarios should consider a design with small tunnels. However, decision makers who are less concerned with worst cases and consider all the futures equally likely might consider large tunnels (39 m³/s). Finally, decision makers concerned with limiting their exposure to extreme dry futures, but who believe those futures to be relatively unlikely, might consider tunnel size between these extremes, in the range of 31–33 m³/s, which, by coincidence, is a capacity close to what would be optimal based on historical climate.

Figure O.10 Reducing Regrets through Robust Adaptation

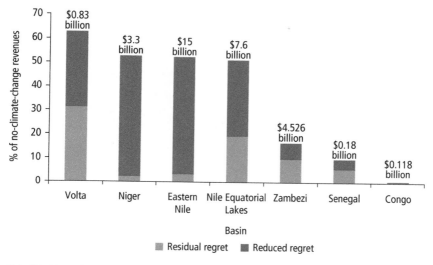

Note: If decision makers ignore climate change and plan investment based on historical climate, they are exposed to the maximum possible damage indicated by the sum of the orange and blue bars (expressed as percentage of reference, no-climate-change revenues). By adopting robust adaptation, the worst-case damage is lower, which is represented by the orange bars. The blue bars thus represent the benefit of adapting, that is, the reduction of worst-case damages. Numbers above the bars indicate the discounted dollar value of adaptation (in terms of reduced maximum regret). The Orange basin is excluded from the adaptation analyses because the Upper Orange geographic study area includes no significant PIDA projects.

Robust adaptation will lead to cost increases when it entails investment in additional generation capacity or enhancements in water-use efficiency; but it could also result in cost savings for facilities that will be downsized to avoid their underutilization in dry climates. In hydropower, cost increases and cost savings appear to be of similar orders of magnitude across basins (figure O.11), mostly in the order of 5–20 percent of baseline investment costs (with the exception of the Niger basin). But cost savings and cost increases do not cancel each other out, because in general, they will accrue to different facilities within each basin and, as a result, to different project developers.

Robust adaptation appears to be fully justified, even when only cost increases are considered (that is, not considering the cost savings of downscaled investments). Comparing the latter with the benefit expressed as a reduction of the maximum regrets, the benefit/cost ratio comfortably exceeds one in all basins (table O.1). The exception is the Congo basin, which confirms that in that basin the regrets from inaction may be too small to warrant significant departures from baseline investment plans.

Figure O.11 Incremental Cost of Robust Adaptation in Hydropower

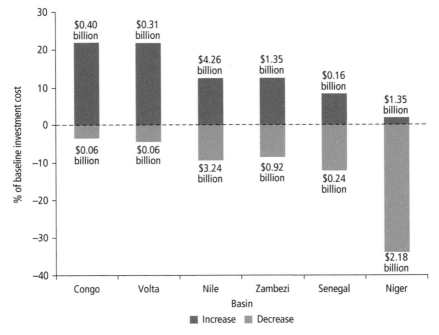

Note: The chart indicates the cost (expressed as a percentage of the baseline investment) of the adaptation strategy that minimizes the maximum regret (regrets are the damages—loss of revenue or missed opportunity to increase it—caused by not selecting the best response to any particular climate). For some of the facilities planned, adaptation will entail cost increases (blue bars); for some others, adaptation might lead to cost decreases or savings (orange bars). Numbers at the top and base of bars indicate the discounted dollar value of cost increases. The Orange basin is excluded from the adaptation analyses because the Upper Orange geographic study area includes no significant PIDA projects.

Table O.1 Costs and Benefits of Robust Adaptation

Basin	Increased cost (US$, billions)	Decreased cost (US$, billions)	Reduced maximum regret (US$, billions)	Benefit/cost ratio
Congo	0.40	0.06	0.12	0.29
Niger	1.35	2.18	3.30	2.45
Nile	4.26	3.24	22.60	5.31
Senegal	0.16	0.24	0.18	1.14
Volta	0.31	0.06	0.83	2.64
Zambezi	1.35	0.92	4.53	3.36

Note: The benefit/cost ratio column shows the reduced maximum regret (the benefits of adaptation) divided by the incremental cost incurred by undertaking adaptation. Because the calculation does not incorporate the cost savings that adaptation brings about for some facilities, it should be considered a conservative, lower-bound estimate. The Orange basin is excluded from the adaptation analyses because the Upper Orange geographic study area includes no significant PIDA projects.

A comprehensive climate change response strategy might include not only ex ante adjustments to investment plans, but also elements of adaptive management, which might help identify additional ways to avoid regrets, through learning as climate change unfolds. For example, in the Volta basin, such an approach would entail an initial reduction in turbine capacity (consistent with the expectation of a dry future), but with the option of adding turbine capacity later, if subsequent information suggests the climate will be wetter. Planners might create such an option by designing the powerhouses and tunnels larger than needed for the initial turbines to reduce the cost of subsequently adding additional turbines.

The findings of the analysis indicate that it is possible, and economically advantageous, to modify investment plans to enable better handling of the risks posed by climate change to the performance of hydropower and irrigation infrastructure (see box O.2 for a more detailed example of the process for the Zambezi River basin).

BOX 0.2

Illustrative Adaptation Results for the Zambezi River Basin

This study provides results for seven basins. It is useful to illustrate the analysis by walking through the key steps and results for a single basin, in this case the Zambezi.

Step 1. Assess the potential for climate change adaptation to alleviate losses and expand opportunities.
If river basin planners knew what future climate change would bring to their region, they could plan infrastructure with "perfect foresight." Although perfect foresight is not possible in reality, it is a useful way to evaluate the potential gains from adaptation efforts. Adaptation in the Zambezi basin has great potential to alleviate losses—avoiding $6.3 billion in potential losses in the driest scenario and accruing $9.1 billion in gains in the wettest one.

Step 2. Assess the regrets of choosing a single adaptation pathway from among the alternatives and look to minimize those regrets.
Although the results of step 1 usefully demonstrate the potential value of adaptation, it is nonetheless important to look at the outcomes of each of these perfect foresight strategies as the planner would, that is, from the perspective that the infrastructure that is built now could ultimately face any of the many possible climate futures. The goal should be to build in a way that minimizes the regret of these choices—the regret of an infrastructure strategy in any future is the difference between its revenues and the revenue of the strategy that performs best in that future. Figure BO.2.1 compares the regret of six alternative specifications of an infrastructure investment plan and the

(continued next page)

Box O.2 (continued)

Figure BO.2.1 Estimates of Regret for Different Adaptation Strategies in the Zambezi Basin

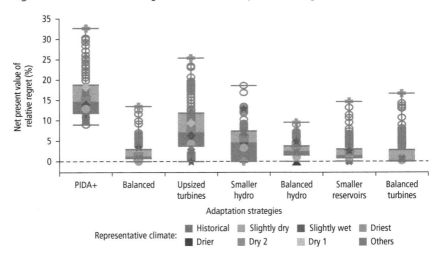

Note: Values are for relative regret. The regret of a strategy in any future is the difference between its performance and the best-performing strategy in that future. That is, the regret measures the difference in net present value (NPV) between the strategy one chooses under uncertainty and the strategy one could have chosen with perfect information about the future. The horizontal axis lists the investment strategies considered in each basin: PIDA+ and the investments generated by the perfect foresight calculations for the six representative climate futures. The vertical axis shows the relative regret for each strategy. The relative regret is a ratio; the numerator is the regret for a particular climate outcome out of the 121 scenarios considered in the analysis (that is, the NPV "penalty" relative to the best possible outcome if the planner had perfect foresight), and the denominator is the NPV for the best possible outcome for that scenario. The colored dots show the regrets for the historical climate and the representative climate futures. Dry 1 and Dry 2 are two representative climates that are close to each other in aridity, drier than Historical and the Slightly Dry, and wetter than the Drier and Driest climates.

no-climate change specification (PIDA+) in the Zambezi basin, across a wide range of climate futures, including ones wetter and drier than the historical climate. In this case, the balanced hydro alternative, third from the right, implies an upsizing of some hydropower projects in the basin and a downsizing of other projects. This combination has the lowest range of regret for each investment alternative, and so represents a robust choice.

Step 3. Evaluate the costs and benefits of a robust adaptation strategy.
Once we have chosen a robust strategy, we can look behind the strategy to estimate the combination of increased costs and cost savings (savings from cases of strategic infrastructure downsizing) and compare those with the benefits of adapting. The last row of table O.1 presents these results—note that the benefit/cost ratio in the table takes a conservative perspective and focuses only on the actual increased costs, but it makes a compelling case that robust adaptation actions can provide economic benefits that are significantly greater than the expected costs.

The specific way in which such modifications should be done, however, depends crucially on attitudes toward risks, time preferences, and the relative priority assigned to the physical performance versus the economic performance of infrastructure, within and across sectors. These are choices that countries and regional organizations will need to make themselves; the results presented in this book are therefore indicative and should not be intended as a substitute for assessments reflecting the full range of stakeholder perspectives and priorities.

Adaptation to Climate Change at the Project Level

To test the applicability at the project level of the approach used at the basin and power pool scales, the book evaluated the sensitivity to climate change of five case study projects and the scope for identifying robust adaptation options.

The case studies span a range of geographic locations (map O.1), current and future climate conditions, and design and management challenges. Project-level

Map O.1 **Location of Case Study Projects**

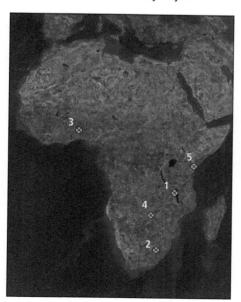

1. Lower Fufu Hydropower Project (Zambezi River basin, Malawi)

2. Polihali Dam and Conveyance Project (Orange River basin, Lesotho)

3. Pwalugu Multi-Purpose Dam Project (Volta River basin, Ghana)

4. Batoka Gorge Hydropower Project (Zambezi River basin, Zambia/Zimbabwe)

5. Mwache Dam and Reservoir Project (Kwale district, Kenya)

performance was assessed over various plausible climate futures to estimate the extent to which key technical and economic metrics of performance are affected. The analysis confirmed that existing designs may be very sensitive to climate change in terms of reduced performance under dry scenarios and potential extra revenues under wet scenarios (figure O.12).

The value added of moving the analysis from the basin to the project level is that additional insights can be obtained by utilizing more information on local circumstances. First, although project performance is in general sensitive to climate change, the project's worthiness is not necessarily affected. In some cases, the benefits and revenues of the project are so high that the risk of negative net present value is low even in extreme future climates. In some cases, variables other than climate may have an even more significant effect on net returns (for example, on price or on demand for power or water).

Figure O.12 Sensitivity to Climate Change of Case Study Projects

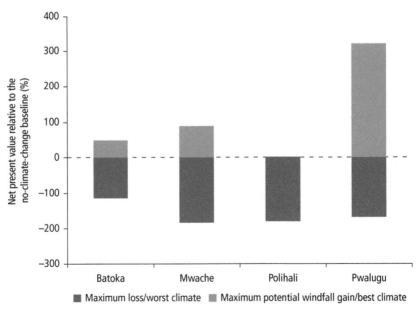

Note: The bars represent the net present value of revenues (for the period 2015–50, discounted at 3 percent) measured relative to the no-climate-change case. Orange bars indicate revenue increases (windfall gains) in the best future climate; blue bars represent revenue losses in the worst future climate.

Figure O.13 Reducing Regrets through Adaptation in Case Study Projects

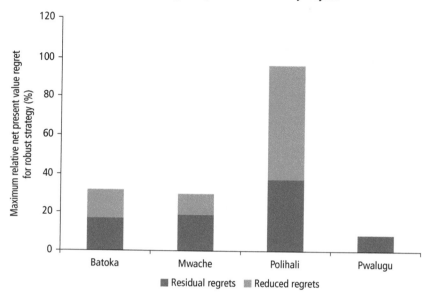

Note: If decision makers ignore climate change and plan investment based on historical climate, they are exposed to the maximum possible damage represented by the sum of the blue and orange bars (expressed as percentage of reference, no-climate-change revenues). By adopting robust adaptation, the worst-case damage is lower, represented by the blue bars. The orange bars thus represent the benefit of adapting. Reduced regrets are those that can be reduced through adapting the project design. Residual regrets are those that cannot be reduced with any adaptation studied for that project—other adaptations may be possible, however, including "soft" adaptations to contractual agreements such as power purchase agreements.

Second, the analysis confirmed that adjustment in project design can reduce regrets. The maximum regret faced by project developers when using existing designs can be cut by 30 percent or more by modifying selected design parameters in anticipation of climate change (figure O.13). But perhaps more importantly, the study found that the scope for adaptation can be considerably broadened if the analysis of climate change impacts is undertaken early in the project design process. This is so because at that early stage, it would be easier to evaluate the relative adaptation benefits of a wider range of interventions, including "hard" engineering parameters (for example, turbine capacity, size of canals, etc.) and "soft" choices, such as the length and terms of performance contracts (for example, power purchasing agreements). Box O.3 provides more details on the analytic process, using the Batoka Gorge project as an illustrative example.

BOX 0.3

Illustrative Adaptation Results for the Batoka Gorge Project

The Batoka Gorge scheme is a hydropower project in the Zambezi River basin, at a site 50 kilometers downstream of Victoria Falls, whose main benefit would be electricity production supplying markets in Zambia and Zimbabwe, within the Southern African Power Pool (SAPP). The resulting power station would have a total installed capacity of 1,600 megawatts, a rated flow of 138.8 cubic meters per second, and produce on average 8,739 gigawatt hours per year, under historical hydrological conditions. This research used Batoka Gorge as an illustrative case study to show the benefits of a robust decision making approach.

Sensitivity and Vulnerability to Climate at the Project Scale

Analysis of the effect of climate change on the performance of Batoka Gorge in terms of hydropower production revealed significant sensitivity to climate change, with up to 33 percent decrease or 15 percent increase in average power production, depending on the climate future. The corresponding dollar value of this range of output variation between the worst and best scenarios is $4 billion in the present value of revenues for the 30-year economic life span, assuming the average cost of power prevailing in the SAPP.

Robust Decision Making and Design at the Project Scale

Looking at a range of different possible designs of the Batoka Gorge project suggests that the maximum regret of building the project a certain way can be reduced by 60–80 percent (depending on regional electricity price levels) compared with the maximum regret if the no-climate-change design were chosen. In this case, as with the other studies in this book, the results are intended to be illustrative only—the results do not imply that the choices made in feasibility studies are incorrect or suboptimal.

For Batoka Gorge, the results also suggest that the design appropriate for the historical climate may be robust over a wide range of climate futures if the design is paired with flexibility in the choice of power contracts. In particular, more nuanced contracts can be used to recoup the costs of larger designs under wet futures and, in dry climates, to redistribute the risks of overbuilding between providers and consumers of power.

Recommendations

Although climate change impacts in the mid-21st century may seem far away, they are going to be very real during the life span of the infrastructure that is being planned now and will be built within the coming decade. If these impacts are not taken into account now, there is a considerable risk to lock the next generation of power and water infrastructure in Africa into designs that could turn out to be inadequate for the climate of the future and costly or impossible to modify later. To avoid that risk, actively promoting integration of climate change in infrastructure development is important at the planning and project levels. For the latter, the approach outlined in this book could be applied beyond the five pilot test cases, considering that the data and analytical requirements are not particularly demanding (box O.4).

But in parallel to further testing the approach in a wider range of locations, there is a need to fully integrate climate change consideration into regular planning and project design processes. And this is likely to require a change in mindset, away from consolidated behavior and practices, with the goal of better integrating the expertise of the relevant professions, such as climate scientists and design engineers. Because such a paradigm shift is likely to have

BOX O.4

What Does It Take to Integrate Climate Change into Project Design?

Implementing the approach proposed in this book at the basin scale—which involves many interactions among the components of a water resource system—is likely to remain complex for some time. But implementation at the project scale has grown more tractable, as suggested by the experience of conducting the case studies presented in this book. The modeling components required for a project-level climate change analysis consist of the following:

- A set of downscaled climate projections for the project's relevant geographic region.

- A hydrologic model of the relevant region, calibrated to local observational records and linked to climate projections that can estimate project inflows and operations for alternative design specifications.

- A simple project design and cost model that can reproduce any existing cost estimates from a pre-feasibility study and can estimate how costs would vary with alternative design specifications. If the complexity of the design precludes the development of a simple design and cost model, several estimates of alternative designs could be developed using more detailed tools.

The requisite sets of climate projections have become increasingly available, including those used for this book. As recommended here, the sets could be provided Africa-wide through a central data repository. Appropriate hydrological modeling platforms have also become increasingly available and can be calibrated using the same data utilized in feasibility studies. Finally, this study has generated a set of project designs and cost models embodied in spreadsheets that can be used as templates for a wide range of applications.

a considerable gestation period, the time to act is now, with priority assigned to the following selected areas for intervention.

1. **Develop technical guidelines on the integration of climate change in the planning and design of infrastructure in climate-sensitive sectors.**

   A multi-stakeholder technical working group could be established to develop voluntary technical guidelines on how to apply the notions of climate resilience, discussed at length in this book, to real-life infrastructure planning and design. The group would include representatives from the development community, relevant professional organizations in the engineering and consulting industries—which could be mobilized through vehicles such as the International Commission on Large Dams—and public sector stakeholders at the regional (for example, Africa Climate Policy Center and New Partnership for Africa's Development) and national levels.

2. **Promote an open-data knowledge repository for climate-resilient infrastructure development.**

   To bring down the cost of the analysis needed to integrate climate considerations into infrastructure development, there is a need to establish common data sources (on climate scenarios, hydrology, standard construction costs, etc.), which could be made available to the public on open-data platforms. These could be hosted by African institutions (such as the Africa Climate Policy Center) and should build on existing platforms (such as the World Bank's Climate Change Knowledge Portal). These knowledge repositories should be updated periodically as new information from the scientific and practitioner communities becomes available. To ensure the credibility of the information provided, suitable vetting mechanisms should be identified (for example, in collaboration with the World Meteorological Organization and the secretariat of the United Nations Framework Convention on Climate Change) so that users will be confident that the data reflect the latest advances of climate science, hydrology, engineering, etc.

3. **Establish an Africa climate resilience project preparation facility.**

   Building on the seed resources made available for the present study, development organizations could mobilize funds to establish a facility that would provide technical assistance for the systematic integration of climate change in the planning and design of Africa's infrastructure. Although eventually climate resilience analysis should become a regular part of program and project preparation, experience on the ground is limited and technical capacity is scarce; it is therefore not realistic that all existing project preparation outfits can rapidly integrate climate stress tests and adaptation analysis into their operations. Instead, it may be preferable to have a dedicated knowledge hub that could provide technical assistance services across the continent for the assessment of climate impacts and particularly for the analysis of adaptation options in project design (including assessment of contracts of service). The facility, to be adequately financed with grant or concessional resources, could have different windows to cater to the specific needs of different sectors, or for different stages of the infrastructure development cycle. For example, the facility could provide support to climate-resilient infrastructure master plans or to the integration of climate resilience into individual projects.

4. **Launch training programs for climate-resilient infrastructure professionals.**

To ensure adequate strengthening of the technical skills that are required to enhance the climate resilience of infrastructure, one or more training programs could be established for professionals involved in the planning, design, and operation of climate-sensitive infrastructures. These could include technical staff of relevant public sector entities (for example, ministries of water, power, and transport; river basin organizations; and power pools) as well as professionals in the academic community and the private sector.

5. **Set up an observatory on climate-resilient infrastructure development in Africa.**

To ensure that the work at the technical level discussed above on methodology, data, project preparation, and training retains visibility and linkages with the policy level of decision making, an observatory on climate-resilient infrastructure development could be established. For example, an observatory could be part of the Infrastructure Consortium for Africa, which is a key platform to catalyze donor and private sector financing of infrastructure projects and programs in Africa, and which already includes climate-resilient infrastructure in its list of priority topics. The Infrastructure Consortium for Africa could operate in partnership with the Africa Climate Policy Center to optimize the distribution of work across areas of comparative advantage.

The observatory could undertake the following activities:

- Keep track of programs and projects featuring significant assessments of climate impacts and adaptation options.
- Monitor trends in financing for climate-resilient infrastructure.
- Help identify the technical, informational, financing, and institutional bottlenecks that prevent progress in integrating climate consideration into infrastructure development.
- Promote a high-level dialogue on possible solutions among decision makers in Africa's national and regional organizations and the international development communities.

Chapter 1

Africa's Power and Water Infrastructure

James E. Neumann

A key ingredient Africa needs to meet its development aspirations is rapid upgrading of the region's infrastructure, which is woefully inadequate in quantity and quality of service. Africa has experienced economic growth of more than 5 percent per annum during the past decade. To sustain this growth, investment in infrastructure is fundamental. The Africa Infrastructure Country Diagnostics (AICD) found that if all African countries were to catch up with Mauritius, the regional leader in infrastructure, per capita growth in the region could increase by 2.2 percentage points (Foster and Briceño-Garmendia 2010).[1] The current poor status of infrastructure is estimated to depress firm productivity by 40 percent. Fixing the problem will not be inexpensive: to enable Africa to fill the infrastructure gap,[2] the AICD found that some US$93 billion per year for the next decade will need to be invested (see box 1.1 for more details).

Understanding of the important place of infrastructure in Africa's development has led to concerted action to plan its scale-up. Most significantly, the Program for Infrastructure Development in Africa (PIDA), endorsed in 2012 by the continent's heads of state and government, lays out an ambitious, long-term plan for closing Africa's infrastructure gap and enabling per capita income to rise above US$10,000 in all the countries of the continent by 2040. To achieve these objectives, PIDA calls for the expansion of highways by 37,000 kilometers (km), hydroelectric power generation capacity by more than 54,000 megawatts, and water storage capacity by 20,000 km³.

Much of this investment will support the construction of long-lived infrastructure (e.g., dams, power stations, and roads), which will need to be capable of delivering services under current and future climate conditions. Although development cooperation agencies and private sector investors are increasingly concerned about the potential vulnerability of infrastructure to the future climate, most of the continent's infrastructure plans (including PIDA) are being

BOX 1.1

Africa Infrastructure Country Diagnostics: Key Findings and Estimated Financing Gaps

The Africa Infrastructure Country Diagnostics (AICD), a study completed in 2010, was designed to expand the knowledge of physical infrastructure in Africa and, in particular, the costs of upgrading African infrastructure to a higher standard. AICD provided a baseline against which future improvements in infrastructure services could be measured and a solid empirical foundation for prioritizing investments and designing policy reforms in the infrastructure sectors in Africa. AICD established an overall economic rationale for this study, including the need to provide new insights on how best to design Africa's path to close the infrastructure gap in the uncertain climate of the future. The synthesis report provides 10 key findings on the priorities of infrastructure investment in Sub-Saharan Africa (Foster and Briceño-Garmendia 2010). The most relevant findings for this study are summarized below.

- **Finding 1.** Infrastructure contributed over half of Africa's improved growth performance. The key implication is that infrastructure is critically important for Africa's development now and in the future.

- **Finding 2.** African countries' infrastructure lags well behind that of other developing countries. Aggressive infrastructure investment plans must be reestablished, including those for long-lived water and power sector investments.

- **Finding 5.** Power is Africa's largest infrastructure challenge by far. This finding reinforces the importance of one of the key focal points for this study, the potentially climate-sensitive hydropower sector. The sector is doubly important in light of the large, untapped hydropower potential of the continent and the desire to grow the electric power sector in renewable and clean energy directions.

- **Finding 6.** Africa's infrastructure spending needs—at US$93 billion a year—are more than double previous estimates by the Commission for Africa. A fresh look at infrastructure needs clarifies the magnitude and urgency of infrastructure investments.

- **Finding 7.** The infrastructure challenge varies greatly by country type. The study acknowledges the need to take a geographically oriented, bottom-up approach, which is also necessary to evaluate climate risks and adaptation opportunities, which also manifest differentially across space.

- **Finding 9.** After potential efficiency gains, Africa's infrastructure funding gap is US$31 billion a year, mostly in the power sector. This finding further establishes the need to assess the climate resiliency of a planned major expansion of hydropower and linked power transmission investments.

(continued next page)

Box 1.1 (continued)

Summary of Infrastructure Financing Gaps by Major Economic Sector as Estimated by the
Africa Infrastructure Country Diagnostics
(US$, billions per year)

Sector	Needs	Spending	Cost of targets minus ongoing spending	Relevant financing gap
Power	42.6	13.8	28.8	28.80
WSS	10.0	5.9	4.1	4.10
Transport	20.3	17.7	2.6	0.10
ICT	1.9	10.0	−8.1	0.10
Irrigation	4.9	0.0	4.9	4.90
Total	79.7	−	−	40.40

Source: Foster and Briceño-Garmendia 2010.
Note: ICT = information and communications technology; WSS = water supply and sanitation; − = not available.

developed largely assuming that historical climate can be used as a guide to
present and future decision making.

The current state of infrastructure planning is the starting point for this
study. To understand how climate change may affect the desirable design,
location, timing, and composition of the stock of infrastructure that will be built
in the future, the study team began by establishing a reference case development
plan. This chapter describes the key elements and conclusions of this major
continent-scale infrastructure effort in the region (PIDA) and an enhanced version of the PIDA plan that takes into account new developments in the region
since PIDA was completed in 2011 and endorsed in 2012. The chapter estab-
lishes a baseline of development benefits of these infrastructure investments,
focused on the climate-sensitive power and water sectors, and provides a road
map for the remainder of the study. The road map shows how climate change
could jeopardize infrastructure investments and the development benefits they
can confer, and outlines a series of adaptations, adjustments, policy changes,
and new or enhanced investments that can mitigate the risks of climate change,
even in the face of significant climate forecasting uncertainty.

The overall objective of the study is to strengthen the analytical base for
investments in Africa's potentially climate-sensitive infrastructure under uncertain future climate—a necessary prerequisite for taking immediate action. More
specifically, the study seeks to accomplish the following:

a) Estimate the effects of projected climate change (chapter 3) on the performance of a subset of infrastructure (chapter 4) over a range of future climate
scenarios (chapter 5)

b) Develop and test a framework for the planning and design of infrastructure investment that can be "robust" under a wide range of climate outcomes (chapters 6 and 7)

c) Help enhance the "investment readiness" of African countries to use climate finance resources geared toward increasing the countries' resilience to climate variability and change

This study is the first to develop a regionwide analysis of the effects of climate change on infrastructure in the power, irrigation, and water supply sectors, with road transport to be analyzed in a separate, future report. The study is also the first to analyze and cost adaptation options, explicitly addressing the constraints imposed by climate uncertainty on the planning and design of infrastructure. The use of a consistent methodology (including the same hydrological and power optimization models and the same set of climate projections) makes the results comparable across the continent's river basins and countries.

PIDA's Key Conclusions

The PIDA program, endorsed in 2012 by African heads of state, provides a stakeholder-driven starting point for the current work, a specific portfolio of investment plans in the water-driven irrigation and hydropower sectors. PIDA stresses transboundary regional integration, with specific reference to water and power infrastructure planning, reinforcing the need for a basin- and power pool–scale approach to assessing the effects of climate change on investment plans. The PIDA framework reflects a vision of sustained economic growth over 30 years and a rise of per capita annual incomes to US$10,000 across the African continent, which will require a rapid upgrade of the region's stock of infrastructure. In line with the AICD findings, the PIDA synthesis document (PIDA 2011) confirms projections of a rapid increase in power demand (from 590 terawatt hours (TWh) in 2010 to more than 3,100 TWh in 2040). To keep pace, the installed power generation capacity of PIDA projects must be increased from the present level of 125 gigawatts (GW) to almost 700 GW in 2040. Meeting this goal will require the rapid deployment of an investment pipeline to avoid gaps in infrastructure supply that could jeopardize the program's overall development vision, including through a loss of international competitiveness in critical economic sectors.

The total estimated cost of implementing all the projects identified by PIDA to address the projected infrastructure needs by 2040 is US$360 billion. The PIDA Priority Action Plan (PAP)—which comprises 51 priority infrastructure backbone projects and programs in energy, information and communications technology, transport, and water—requires investment of US$68 billion to be realized by 2020. By far, the largest demand for investment is for energy, accounting for US$40.3 billion, or 60 percent of the PIDA PAP program, followed by transport at US$25.4 billion or 37 percent. Africa's vast, untapped hydropower potential is reflected in PIDA's plans for energy sector development, as shown in map 1.1.

Map 1.1 Summary of PIDA Energy Infrastructure Development Proposals and Priorities

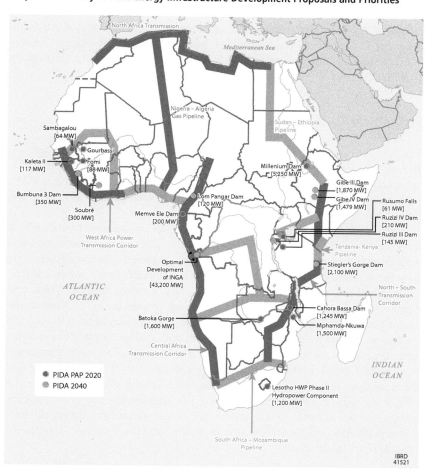

Source: Programme for Infrastructure Development in Africa: Interconnecting, Integrating and Transforming a Continent, PIDA, http://www.afdb.org/en/topics-and-sectors/initiatives-partnerships /programme-for-infrastructure-development-in-africa-pida/.
Note: The infrastructure scenario used in the current study includes PIDA hydropower and storage projects that lie in the seven river basins in the study's scope. The study also includes irrigation and additional hydropower projects not included in PIDA (e.g., the proposed Mambila hydropower plant in the Niger basin in Nigeria). HWP = Highlands Water Project; INGA = Inga 3 and Grand Inga hydropower projects; MW = megawatts; PAP = Priority Action Plan; PIDA = Program for Infrastructure Development in Africa.

The PIDA energy infrastructure program focuses on major hydroelectric projects and interconnections of power pools to meet the forecasted increase in electricity demand. Thus, the program reflects two of the main focus areas of this study: irrigation infrastructure and additional hydropower projects that supplement PIDA, constituting the PIDA+ reference scenario described in chapter 4. Of the US$40.3 billion in the PIDA energy sector PAP, US$21.3 billion is for hydropower projects (all the major hydropower projects are included in the scope of this study), and US$18.9 billion is to enhance electric transmission capability. The former is potentially climate-sensitive and is a focus of this work; the latter is potentially one of the best ways to build resilience to climate-induced shocks to the water sector, which are unlikely to occur simultaneously over the full range of Sub-Saharan Africa.

Scope and Time Horizon of the Study

The scope of the study includes the power, irrigation, and water supply sectors. The sectors were selected based on their strategic role in Africa's overall development, as expressed by most stakeholders; the results of the AICD and PIDA work summarized above; and the sectors' sensitivity to climate variability and future changes.

The geographic units of the analysis are river basins and power pools, which represent natural aggregations for planning for water-related investment and integrated power systems. The analysis focuses on the seven river basins that have the greatest strategic significance for the continent's hydropower and irrigation potential, namely, the Congo, Niger, Nile, Orange, Senegal, Volta, and Zambezi. As shown in map 1.2, the scope of the Orange basin is limited to the Upper Orange, above the confluence with the Vaal, consistent with input from the Orange-Senqu River basin Authority. But since no significant PIDA projects are in that portion of the Orange basin, the analysis for the Orange basin focuses on climate impacts on the stock of *existing* infrastructure. For the other basins, the focus is on *planned new infrastructure*. Together the basins account for the bulk of the region's development potential, including some 200 GW of hydropower generation capacity. The power infrastructure analysis covers the four power pools in Sub-Saharan Africa, namely, the Southern, Central, Eastern, and West African Power Pools.

Value Added of the Report

The implications of climate change for development (in Africa and other regions) have received a significant amount of attention in the literature in

Map 1.2 Selected River Basins and Power Pools in Africa

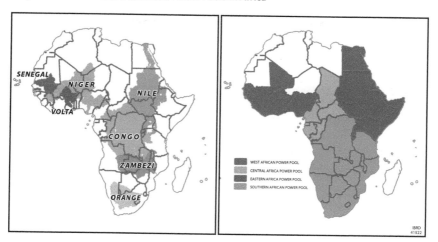

recent years (see box 1.2). Previous studies have yielded important insights to guide planning for climate-resilient infrastructure, but have necessarily focused on a limited geographic scale (e.g., a single basin), a limited sector scale (e.g., water but not hydropower), or a limited set of climate futures (e.g., a handful of future scenarios). The present study adds to the existing knowledge base in the following ways:

- Some studies have covered certain sectors throughout the African continent, but with inadequate (or missing) treatment of important sectors, such as power or irrigation. This study looks at hydropower, non-hydro sources of power, and irrigation in a consistent, multi-basin framework.

- Some studies have provided more complete coverage of subsectors for a few countries or only one basin (see box 1.2 for an example). This study examines seven major river basins across Sub-Saharan Africa.

- Most studies have proven that climate adaptation is fundamental in Africa's water and power sectors, but have not provided specific information on what can be done (the Niger basin study described in box 1.2 is a notable exception). This study buttresses the conclusion that climate adaptation is fundamental for Africa, with specific, quantitative estimates of the potential for adaptation to improve infrastructure performance. The study also illustrates a clear methodology at the basin and project levels, which, with

BOX 1.2

Key Previous Studies on Climate Change and Infrastructure in Africa

Niger Basin: Climate Risk Assessment (CRA) for the Sustainable Development Action Plan

The Niger basin study provides an excellent example of a well-executed climate change "stress test" that is then used to develop climate adaptation options for the water sector. The Sustainable Development Action Plan (SDAP) provides a planned infrastructure investment starting point to examine vulnerability. The global climate models in the climate risk assessment (CRA) project used only modest changes in precipitation over the basin (mostly between −6 and +7 percent, on average +2 percent), while all climate models project significant increases in temperature, mostly between 1.50°C and 30°C for 2050 (on average 2.10°C or 8 percent). The average projected decline in runoff is about 2 percent; most models project an average change in runoff between −18 and +10 percent. The current water allocation rules in the Niger basin SDAP prioritize irrigated agriculture to secure food production and alleviate poverty, making the plan insensitive to projected climate changes. Some agricultural production decreases may occur, but would generally be less than 3 percent of the output projected for SDAP. Climate change impacts on hydro energy, navigation, and flooding of the Niger Inner Delta are projected to be mild (< 10 percent decrease) to moderate (< 20 percent decrease).

These impacts can be reduced by reducing rainy season irrigated agriculture or by the construction of additional storage reservoirs along with hydro energy generation facilities in the water-producing parts of the basin (in the Upper Niger basin and in Nigeria). SDAP and particularly the construction of the Fomi and Kandadji Dams constitute an effective adaptation to climate change impacts on SDAP itself, because of the abundance of water resources in the rainy season and the creation of large water storage areas for dry season water supply for irrigation and the sustenance of minimum flows. In addition, the development of run-of-the-river hydropower plants can significantly improve the rate of return on SDAP investments without affecting energy generation at downstream hydropower plants.

Zambezi Basin: Multi-Sector Investment Opportunities Analysis and Related Studies

The Multi-Sector Investment Opportunities Analysis (MSIOA) provides an example of a stakeholder-driven, basin-scale investment analysis that includes consideration of multi-sector trade-offs in water resource investments (hydropower and irrigated agriculture). The initial study explored these trade-offs to hone the investment strategy and balance hydropower and irrigation investments with consideration of economic returns, employment implications, and flood control. In a follow-on study, a more detailed look at climate change was conducted. That assessment focused on evaluation, in light of potential future climate change, of one investment scenario of interest,

(continued next page)

Box 1.2 (continued)

which reflected a gradual increase in irrigation-equipped area based on existing national plans and programs, together with development of new hydropower plants in accordance with a plan put forward by the Southern African Power Pool. MSIOA incorporated a static assessment of the effects of climate change on this scenario, based on a few scenarios of changes in air temperature (affecting reservoir evaporation) and estimates of in-stream flow derived from other work. The follow-on study demonstrated how a more rigorous assessment of a full range of possible climate change outcomes for the region, including monthly temperature, precipitation, and runoff estimates, could affect outcomes. The analysis yielded the following key insights:

- Returns to hydropower and irrigation investments would be significantly affected by climate change, in virtually all areas of the Zambezi Basin, by as much as 10 percent basin-wide by 2030, and by 35 percent basin-wide by 2050.

- The greatest risks to hydropower are in the Upper Zambezi region, which includes Kariba Dam, and the Kafue River region, which includes Kafue Gorge hydropower. Climate change also presents significant risks to irrigation investments. Unmet irrigation demands for the dry scenario were found to be as high as 15 percent early in the century and 22 percent by mid-century in the Zambezi at the Cahora Bassa and Lower Zambezi sub-basins, above and beyond those projected for the baseline climate scenario.

Nile Basin: Nile Basin Initiative Climate Change Strategy

The Nile Basin Initiative (NBI) Climate Change Strategy was developed as stipulated in the Nile Basin Sustainability Framework under its Key Strategic Direction 4: "Climate Change Adaptation & Mitigation." The Climate Change Strategy forms an integral part of the landscape of NBI policies, strategies, and guidelines. The strategy complements the national efforts of NBI member countries. The strategy focuses on transboundary water resource management as a strategic element of climate adaptation and low-carbon development in the region. The strategy was informed by sub-basin-level studies commissioned by the NBI on climate change effects on water resources and the socioeconomic development of the region, vulnerabilities to climate change, appropriate coping measures, and feasible development options. The comprehensive regional assessment carried out by the Eastern Nile Technical Regional Office, the MSIOA carried out by the Nile Equatorial Lakes Subsidiary Action Program Coordination Unit (NELSAP-CU), specific basin monographs prepared by NELSAP-CU, and the basin-wide climate change assessment carried out by the Water Resources Planning and Management project were of particular relevance. Furthermore, the "State of the River Nile Basin Report 2012" (NBI 2012), which consolidated scientific findings on the effects of climate change in the Nile region, informed the development of the strategy. The main outcomes of the strategy focus on establishing the capability to identify, finance, and implement adaptation options in vulnerable areas.

Sources: NBA and World Bank 2013; World Bank 2010; Strzepek et al. 2011; SADC and ZRA 2008; NBI 2012.

appropriate capacity-building assistance, can provide specific guidance for adaptation strategies.

• Only a few studies have explicitly addressed the issue of how to use the results of impact analysis to inform investment decisions in conditions of deep uncertainty about the future climate; none has provided a consistent framework across multiple basins in Sub-Saharan Africa. In most cases, the assumption of "perfect foresight" for adapting to climate change has been implicitly employed in previous studies; a formal assessment of robustness has not been employed. This study provides one of the first comprehensive tests of a robust decision-making framework for Africa.

Limitations of the Analysis

A study with a geographic scope that encompasses all of Sub-Saharan Africa, over a time frame spanning the next 35 years, necessarily implies some limitations in coverage. The impact of climate change on hydropower, irrigation, and power pool performance is most directly linked to uncertain estimations of river flow volumes, the focus in this work. Other environmental factors can affect infrastructure performance, however, and some of those factors may be linked to climate change. For example, sedimentation is an important issue in reservoir-based water projects, but there remains little detailed science and hydrologic information so far on the impacts of climate change on sedimentation rates. Further, although sedimentation is an important issue in the Blue Nile, the Nile below Khartoum, and some other regions of Africa, as a whole, sedimentation rates are less an issue in this geographic area than in other areas worldwide.

Another effect that has been linked to climate change is flooding, which also can be mitigated by infrastructure design and planning. A few of the reservoir projects considered in the project-scale analysis, for example, include flood control benefits in the feasibility studies. Flooding and sedimentation events take place at the sub-monthly scale, however, and so cannot be reliably addressed with the monthly timescale adopted for this study. Groundwater might be an important irrigation source in some regions and could be part of a broader adaptation strategy, but it is not linked to hydropower performance. A study of groundwater would require specialized tools and data collection; therefore, it was omitted from the scope of the analysis. Nonetheless, sedimentation, flooding, and groundwater resources are all important water resource management issues for Africa and deserve attention in future work.

Notes

1. AICD is a multi-stakeholder partnership that incorporates various donors under the leadership of the African Union Commission and other key regional organizations. During 2006–10, AICD developed a comprehensive repository of analysis and knowledge on Africa's infrastructure in the electricity, water, roads, and information and communications technology sectors.
2. The gap is defined as the distance between the current quantity and quality of infrastructure and a set of sector-specific targets that, if achieved, would enable Africa to catch up with the rest of the developing world. These targets include the Millennium Development Goals for water and connectivity between all key economic nodes (cities, ports, borders, secondary towns, and agriculturally productive areas), supply-demand balance for power, steady progress on electrification, and universal access to the Global System for Mobile Communications and WiMAX telecenters.

References

Foster, Vivien, and Cecilia Briceño-Garmendia, eds. 2010. *Africa's Infrastructure: A Time for Transformation*. Washington, DC: Agence Française de Développement and World Bank. http://www.infrastructureafrica.org/aicd/library/doc/552/africa%E2%80%99s-infrastructure-time-transformation.

NBA (Niger Basin Authority) and World Bank. 2013. "Niger River Basin Sustainable Development Action Plan: Niger River Basin Climate Risk Assessment for the Sustainable Development Action Plan." Summary report. World Bank, Washington, DC.

NBI (Nile Basin Initiative Secretariat). 2012. *State of the River Nile Basin 2012*. Entebbe, Uganda. http://nileis.nilebasin.org/content/state-river-nile-basin-report.

PIDA (Program for Infrastructure Development in Africa). 2011. "Study on Programme for Infrastructure Development in Africa (PIDA) Phase III: PIDA Study Synthesis." SOFRECO Led Consortium. African Union, Addis Ababa, Ethiopia.

SADC (South African Development Community) and ZRA (Zambezi River Authority). 2008. *Integrated Water Resources Management Strategy and Implementation Plan for the Zambezi Basin*. http://www.zambezicommission.org/downloads/Zambezi%20River%20Basin%20IWRM%20Strategy%20ZAMSTRAT.pdf.

Strzepek, Kenneth, Alyssa McCluskey, Brent Boehlert, Michael Jacobsen, and Charles Fant IV. 2011. "Assessment of the Impacts of Climate Change on Multi-Sector Investment Opportunities in the Zambezi River Basin." World Bank, Washington, DC.

World Bank. 2010. "The Zambezi River Basin: A Multi-Sector Investment Opportunity Analysis. (MSIOA)." Water Resources Management, Africa Region, World Bank, Washington, DC. http://documents.worldbank.org/curated/en/2010/06/13236172/zambezi-river-basin-multi-sector-investment-opportunities-analysis-vol-1-4-summary-report.

of climate change. The illustrative assumption is "perfect foresight" about which of the many climate futures will actually unfold. The methodology is described below.

4. Acknowledging that the uncertainty in climate change is deep (and therefore precludes perfect foresight). The final step consists of identifying a "robust" adaptation alternative, that is, one that provides resilience to the broadest possible range of forecasted climate changes, minimizing the regrets of fixing infrastructure plans in advance of knowing how the future will unfold.

Track 1: Analysis of Climate Change Impacts and Adaptation at the Planning Stage

For each river basin and power pool, the study evaluates the cost of climate change impacts and the merits of adaptation using the framework summarized in table 2.1, which illustrates the approach. The starting point is the reference case, Case A, in which the PIDA+ investment plan is carried out, with a certain cost, and with benefits proxied by the present value of revenues accruing from

Table 2.1 Framework for Evaluating the Impacts of Climate Change on the Energy Sector

Case ID	Case description	Investment strategy	Assumptions on climate	Adaptation strategy	Cost of climate change impacts
A	Reference case	PIDA+	Historical climate (no climate change)	None	Zero
B	Climate change, no adaptation	PIDA+	Full range of climate futures	None	For each climate future, reduction or increase in hydropower performance + reduction or increase in irrigated agriculture performance
C	Climate change, perfect foresight adaptation	PIDA+ with perfect foresight (varies across scenarios)	A representative set of six climate futures that spans the full range of climate futures	Adjust PIDA+ to maximize (for each climate future) the net present value of adaptations	Costs minimized to the limits of adaptation potential under perfect foresight; therefore, the cost represents residual impacts remaining after adaptation options are exhausted
D	Climate change, robust adaptation	PIDA+ with robust adaptation (does not vary across scenarios)	Full range of climate futures (for six representative climate adaptation strategies)	Choose from among the six Case C strategies to manage regrets across climate futures	Reduced compared with the no-adaptation situation (Case B) case performance

the operation of infrastructure, namely from hydropower generation and the value of irrigated crops. If climate change occurs, but no adaptation takes place, Case B materializes: no adaptation is undertaken, PIDA+ is implemented as planned, and regrets can occur. In dry scenarios, the regrets take the form of lost hydropower production, higher cost of electric power to consumers, and lower irrigated crop production, compared with the reference case. In wet scenarios, the regrets consist of forgone opportunities for higher power production, lower costs of electric power, and higher irrigated crop production.

Note that additional flow does not always result in an increase in hydropower. As is true "on the ground," hydropower infrastructure has limits, and in some cases an increase in water can exceed the unit's capacity, leading to water routed to the spillway (and a potentially lost opportunity for hydropower production). In addition, higher rainfall does not always lead to higher river flows—the combined effect of higher rainfall and higher temperature, not uncommon in climate scenarios, also implies higher evaporation and evapotranspiration rates, which can lead to no net change or even a decline in river runoff and, hence, in hydropower production potential. Detailed analysis of the effects would require the use of a detailed, systems-type infrastructure model to estimate the effects of changed river flow on hydropower performance. The use of such a model goes beyond the scope of the present study.

Case C is a counterfactual introduced to gauge the cost of inaction and the benefits of adaptation action. It is a "perfect foresight" situation in which the PIDA+ is optimized to achieve the best possible performance of the energy system in each climate future. Case C corresponds to a hypothetical situation in which investment planners know in advance which climate will unfold and decide accordingly ex ante how the reference scenario (PIDA+) should be adjusted (for example, installing more hydro in wet scenarios or less in drier ones).

The final case, Case D, is the definition of a "robust" adaptation strategy, which requires establishing the options in Case C as a prerequisite, as a sort of "menu" of discrete adaptation strategies to test for resilience to climate change. In Case D, a modification of the reference investment strategy is adopted. This cannot be the "optimal" plan identified in Case C, since the future is unknown. If we could confidently associate probabilities to individual futures, a traditional risk assessment paradigm could be employed. But climate scientists are limited in their ability to associate probabilities to the various climate models, so it remains difficult to know which models may be more likely to be correct—as a result, the model outcomes are all plausible and none is more likely than any other. Therefore, the adaptation strategy chosen in Case D is one that yields acceptable outcomes in as many climate futures as possible. By comparing Case D (robust adaptation) with Cases B and C, the study provides an indication of the potential for reducing the regrets (i.e., the benefits of adaptation) and the costs of doing so. Of course, the definition of "acceptable outcomes" cannot be identified by analysts alone—so for the purposes of this report, several decision rules for managing regrets are tested and compared.

For some components of the Track 1 analysis, in particular, to estimate perfect foresight adaptations for Case C, the study team needed to focus on a few representative climate futures. This small set of futures should provide a good sample of the range of consequences implied by the full range of the climate futures used in the Case B vulnerability analysis (see chapter 3). Given the computational and analyst time involved with each perfect foresight calculation, the study team was able to conduct six such calculations for each of the seven river basins. The process for identifying an appropriate representative set of six, from among all the alternative climate futures in our ensemble (see chapter 3) is described in online appendix E and the outcomes are described in chapter 3. In summary, the process involves using an indicator, the Climate Moisture Index, which combines precipitation and temperature and is reasonably well correlated with the hydropower and irrigation impacts expected from each climate projection, to find a set of consistently wet and dry climate futures across the seven basins under analysis.

Reference Case

The development baseline included in the reference case reflects continent-wide priorities as expressed in PIDA, as well as subregional and national investment plans, resulting in PIDA+. Further details on the establishment of the baseline are provided in chapter 4. The economic analysis of the reference scenario provides a base case from which the impacts of climate change and the costs and benefits of adaptation are measured. In chapter 4, the cost of the reference case investments is estimated to provide the context for the overall analysis, but the baseline from which adaptation benefits are measured is the present value of infrastructure performance—that is, revenues from hydropower production and revenues from irrigated agricultural production. The purpose of this study is not to evaluate PIDA, or the PIDA+ reference case, but to evaluate adaptation—so no benefit-cost analysis of PIDA or PIDA+ is conducted. Instead, the present value of infrastructure performance is the appropriate baseline against which the benefits of adaptation are assessed.

The adaptation analysis does adopt a benefit-cost framework, however. When assessing the benefits and costs of adaptation, a net present value calculation is used, reflecting changes in the revenues from infrastructure performance, as well as the costs of adapting that infrastructure to be better tuned to future climate.

Estimation of Costs and Benefits

The analysis estimates the present value economic benefits of adopting the reference case under historical climate in Case A, the economic impacts of climate change for Case B, and the net benefits of adaptation for Cases C and D. For Case B, the study team estimated impacts as the differences in future basin-wide irrigation and hydropower present value revenues for each of 121 climate futures (see chapter 3) relative to the Case A (reference) scenario revenues. Present value revenues in Cases A and B assume the PIDA+ infrastructure plan is followed with no modifications between 2010 and 2050. As a result, the physical impacts in the Case B scenarios are composed of changes in hydropower production and crop yields under each of the climate change scenarios. For each of the climate futures evaluated under Case C, the study team estimated the net benefits of adaptation as the difference between total present value revenues with and without perfect foresight (i.e., with and without modifications from PIDA+), less (plus) any present value infrastructure costs (savings) of adaptation. So these calculations involve four components: hydropower and irrigation revenues, and hydropower and irrigation infrastructure adaptation costs. The first two components apply to all four cases, and the last two apply to Cases C and D, because in these cases the baseline PIDA+ reservoir and irrigation infrastructure costs are modified.

The present value and net present value calculations reflect implementation of the PIDA+ or alternative infrastructure scenarios over the period 2015 to 2050, using a discount rate of 3 percent. This central rate recommendation is consistent with recent thinking on climate change analysis, reflecting a social welfare–equivalent discount rate that is appropriate for a study that focuses on infrastructure planning and assesses an infrastructure program's benefits from a social welfare perspective. More details are provided in box 2.1.

The tools and data used in the study include a wide range of integrated, consistent climate futures for Sub-Saharan Africa with the latest techniques for interpreting the results of general circulation models (see chapter 3 and online appendix E); physical effects models to estimate monthly river flow and the balance between water supply and demand in the seven major river basins (Water Evaluation and Planning [WEAP] system model; see online appendix C); and updated power pool electric generation planning tools (Open Source Energy Modeling System [OSeMOSYS] model; see online appendix D). The full range of data sources utilized for the analysis is spelled out in online appendix G.

An overview of the process flow for these modeling tools is provided in figure 2.1. Specifically, hydropower production data from the seven basin analyses are fed into the energy models, which then run an optimization routine to estimate an electric energy price trajectory for the reference case infrastructure.[1]

BOX 2.1

Discount Rates

A discount rate of 3 percent is used throughout the Track 1 analysis. This value is consistent with recent thinking on climate change analyses. There are essentially two distinct concepts for discount rates: a social welfare–equivalent discount rate appropriate for determining whether a given policy would augment social welfare (according to a postulated social welfare function) and a finance-equivalent discount rate suitable for determining whether the policy would offer a potential Pareto improvement. Different rates can be used in these two situations.

For the Track 1 analysis, the use of a higher finance-equivalent rate might be justified. The cost of private capital in Africa is typically quite high, perhaps as a result of the inefficient finance sector and the high overall growth rate. A high cost of capital can be justified by high-productivity capital—but it is not clear that those conditions apply broadly in Africa or, in particular, in the case of the large, and largely public, infrastructure projects considered in this study. Further, lower rates are typically justified when evaluating options over longer time frames, as is done in the study. The 3 percent rate chosen for the study rests in part on these types of arguments. The tools developed allow for sensitivity tests using 5 percent and 1 percent alternatives, which bracket reasonable rates for longer-term financial and social welfare–equivalent rates over our time period. The results of the sensitivity tests are described further in the online appendixes.[a]

The test project analyses in Track 2 (chapter 7) reflect project-level financing constraints on the costs of capital through the application of an assumed interest rate on all capital expenditures. The rate used is 10 percent, with some specific exceptions made for projects where this cost of capital appeared too high.[b] The analyses also consider the preferences of net benefits over time from a social welfare perspective by applying a discount rate to future net benefits. The project team explored the sensitivity of social discount rates by using values of 0, 3, and 5 percent, but present results for 3 percent in the test projects. Further details on the Track 2 approach are provided in chapter 7.

a. Appendixes are available online at https://openknowledge.worldbank.org/handle/10986/21875.
b. Further information on project-specific background analysis is available upon request to the editors (rcervigni@worldbank.org).

The resulting prices, along with a crop price trajectory derived from the International Food Policy Research Institute (IFPRI) (Nelson et al. 2010), are used to estimate the economic impacts.

Hydropower revenue is total annual hydropower generation from WEAP multiplied by annual hydropower producer prices. Annual producer hydropower prices are assumed to be the levelized costs of electricity (from the OSeMOSYS model) multiplied by 1.25, where the 1.25 multiplier reflects the fact that producers' revenues are expected to exceed levelized costs by

Figure 2.1 Schematic of Model Interactions to Estimate the Cost of Climate Change to Infrastructure

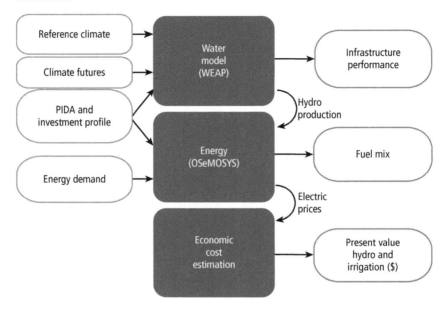

Note: OSeMOSYS = Open Source Energy Modeling System; PIDA = Program for Infrastructure Development in Africa; WEAP = Water Evaluation and Planning system.

approximately a 25 percent margin. OSeMOSYS prices are based on a detailed optimization to minimize levelized electricity costs over an entire power pool, over the full modeling period (2010 to 2050), utilizing the full range of possible electricity sources available to the power pool planner (e.g., hydropower, fossil, nuclear, renewables, diesel, etc.); details are provided in online appendix D.

Irrigation revenues are crop revenues per hectare for each crop multiplied by the number of hectares of each crop across the basin. Crop revenues are annual yields multiplied by the annual consumer crop prices. Consumer crop prices are taken from IFPRI, which provides crop- and country-specific forecasts of crop prices through 2050 (Nelson et al. 2010). Admittedly, it is a limitation of the analysis that these crop price projections are not sensitive to climate scenarios—in dry scenarios, for example, we would expect that local prices would increase and thus the economic productivity of the remaining, viable irrigated areas would increase. The adoption of a small, open economy assumption, using world market prices, which by definition are not responsive to local weather, simplifies the analysis. A more complete treatment of the quantity-price interaction at the domestic level would have required a major additional analytical effort. Instead, the project team determined that it was more important to concentrate the limited resources available on endogenizing energy prices, through use of the power pool modeling. Nonetheless, the impact of the simplified agricultural price approach on the results is likely to be limited for the following reason: Under a dry climate, typically there will be a drop in production and thus a negative effect on the revenues of irrigated crops. In principle, this could be partly offset by a positive effect, to the extent that lower supply leads to higher prices and thus an increase in revenues. Which of the two effects dominates will depend on the price elasticity of demand.[2]

Maximum crop yields are from the Food and Agriculture Organization (FAO), and are assumed to rise by 1 percent each year because of technological advancements. Actual crop yields are the sum of rainfed yields (i.e., the component of total yield that would occur regardless of irrigation) and yields specifically attributable to irrigation water application. Rainfed crop yields are the maximum yield adjusted based on (a) the ratio of effective precipitation to total consumptive crop water demand and (b) the crop-water response factor (from FAO 1998). Effective precipitation is the depth of precipitation that is available for consumptive crop use, and is calculated using procedures outlined by IFPRI (Nelson et al. 2010). The component of total actual yields attributable to irrigation is based on the ratio of total irrigation water deliveries to total irrigation water demand, adjusted based on irrigation efficiency and deficit irrigation (in Case C). For hydropower and irrigation, annual revenues are then discounted to generate present value benefits in Cases A, B, and C.

The perfect foresight modeling for Case C allows several changes in reservoir and irrigation infrastructure: (a) hydropower turbine capacity, (b) reservoir storage capacity, (c) total planned irrigated area, and (d) field and conveyance irrigation efficiency. Costs or savings (capital and operations and maintenance) from changes in hydropower turbine capacity and reservoir storage capacity are estimated by first disaggregating total planned hydropower facility costs (from a variety of sources) into hydroelectric and reservoir components, and then applying simplified exponential functional forms from the literature that relate changes in storage and turbine capacity to changes in total costs (see online appendixes A and B for information on these data sources, which are mostly feasibility studies for similar projects). In the case of planned run-of-the-river facilities, adaptation costs (but not investment costs) are assumed to be part of the hydroelectric infrastructure. The savings from reductions in irrigated area are simply the total change in hectares multiplied by the average capital and operations and maintenance costs of a new irrigated hectare. (Consistent with the objective function described above, Case C assumes that planned irrigated area cannot increase from PIDA+, as once food security is established, water is allocated to hydropower.) Capital costs are the average per hectare expenditures on successful irrigation projects in Sub-Saharan Africa from the International Water Management Institute (IWMI). Irrigation efficiency costs are divided into on-farm technology improvements and conveyance costs, where on-farm improvements are based on IWMI estimates of Sub-Saharan Africa's per-hectare irrigation costs, and conveyance costs are based on the cost of two levels of canal improvements (lining earthen canals and replacement with concrete canals) based on estimates from FAO and the Irrigation Training and Research Center.

Perfect Foresight Adaptation

The perfect foresight Case C approach is a data and computationally intensive step in the overall methodology. As a result, it is performed on a limited set of six scenarios, selected by the study team to span the range of relevant climate outcomes within the study basins and across Sub-Saharan Africa. The objective of this step of the approach is to maximize the difference of present value of benefits less the present value of marginal adaptation costs to expand or contract infrastructure plans. The change in infrastructure plans is measured relative to the reference PIDA+ investment plan. This optimization problem has a significant set of constraints on the options for adaptation.

The overall objective function used in this analysis is the maximization of the net present value of hydropower production, an energy resource that is abundant in much of Sub-Saharan Africa and yet largely untapped. To reflect the political importance of competing uses of water, this objective is assumed to be subject to the constraint of allocating water to environmental flows, municipal use, industrial demands, and irrigation, in that order of priority, which is consistent with stakeholder-driven assessments, such as the recent Multi-Sector Investment Opportunities Analysis of the Zambezi basin.[3]

Adaptation is focused on the planned infrastructure of PIDA+ and not on the autonomous adaptations that farmers and power system managers will make to decadal climate variability. As such, the adaptation plans do not include changes to existing irrigation areas, but allow for changes in irrigation efficiency and crops on existing irrigated areas to allow for national-scale agricultural production adaptation that includes constrained imports as one option.

The other adaptation options that are considered include expansion of turbine capacity at existing hydropower facilities (as power plant expansions are actual PIDA projects being analyzed) and increases and decreases in turbine capacity at PIDA+ planned projects. The options do not include changes in the size of existing reservoirs or increases in the maximum size of planned reservoirs. It is assumed that reservoirs are designed in the reference case at or near their maximum physical capacity with reference to topography constraints. However, the adaptation analysis does allow for reduction in the size of planned storage projects, to avoid over-design of investment in dry scenarios. These assumptions are reasonable for a basin-scale planning study, but the option to increase or decrease storage size in some projects is certainly plausible, and should be considered where possible in project-scale adaptation analyses. A summary of the adaptation levers is provided in table 2.2. The cost functions used for these adaptation measures are derived from the literature and other analyses, which are documented in online appendixes B and G.

The goals of adaptation are different under the wet and dry scenarios. Under dry scenarios, the goal is to recover as much of the lost benefits from climate change as possible without spending more than the amount of the recovered benefits. Under wet scenarios, the goal is to take advantage of the increase in water resources, up to the level where the marginal benefits of additional power or crop production equal the marginal costs of additional infrastructure.

Figure 2.2 is a schematic representation of the two-stage optimization methodology, which implements the framework presented in the section above.

Table 2.2 Adaptation Levers in the Perfect Foresight Modeling

Decision variable	Application to facilities	Range of lever modification
Basin level		
Planned turbine capacity	New, PIDA+ hydropower facilities	The capacity of each new facility can be modified in the following increments: −50%, −25%, 0%, +25%, +50%.
Planned reservoir storage	New hydropower and multiple-use facilities	Reservoirs cannot be made larger than their planned size in the PIDA+ profile, because of engineering constraints. But new facilities can be made smaller than planned, by either −50% or −25%.
Mean conveyance irrigation efficiency	All basins with new irrigation water distribution	At the basin scale, irrigation efficiency can be improved in increments of 10%, from a baseline assumption of 75% conveyance efficiency, to 85% or 95%. The implied approach to improving efficiency is lining and/or covering conveyance canals and other infrastructure to reduce losses.
Farm level		
Planned irrigated area	All new PIDA+ irrigation schemes	The size of PIDA+ irrigation schemes can be adjusted on a continuous basis from −50% to +50%.
Mean deficit irrigation (of water requirements)	All new PIDA+ irrigation schemes	A deficit irrigation strategy can be deployed, which decreases yields but in a nonlinear way. Options include deficit irrigation of 30%, 20%, 10%, or 0%.
Mean field-level irrigation efficiency	All new PIDA+ irrigation schemes	At the field level, irrigation efficiency is assumed to be 60% in the reference case, corresponding with traditional flood irrigation techniques, but can be increased to 70% or 80% through investments in such technologies as laser-leveling or sprinkler irrigation.
Annual crop imports (of total production)	All new PIDA+ irrigation schemes	As a stopgap measure, to maintain overall agricultural production at the basin level, crops can be imported, at a price equivalent to that for the International Food Policy Research Institute's world market prices (which are higher than local prices).

Figure 2.2 Two-Stage Optimization Scheme

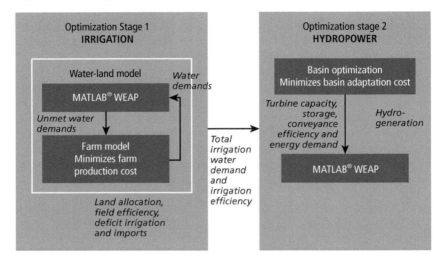

Note: MATLAB® = A high-level language and interactive environment for numerical computation, visualization, and programming; WEAP = Water Evaluation and Planning.

The irrigation optimization stage comes first, because the availability of water for irrigation operates as a constraint in the WEAP modeling—the objective function effectively seeks to maximize hydropower production subject to the constraint that agricultural production be maintained at the level defined by the first-stage optimization. The methodology effectively acknowledges the importance of food security policies for African governments.

Hydropower production is part of a national multi-fuel electric grid and a regional power pool grid. The impact of climate change on the magnitude and timing of the hydropower generated may change the optimal fuel type capacity and generation mix nationally and/or at the power pool level. This changes the levelized cost and thus the opportunity costs of lost hydropower or the returns associated to additional hydropower production in the basin. This change in desired hydropower supply is exogenous to the WEAP model. The second stage of the optimization approach analyzes the economics of the hydro generation expansion or contraction, under the constraint of holding irrigation and other water uses constant. Note that the optimization does not trade off agricultural production for hydropower or vice versa, but seeks to meet a stylized food security constraint before maximizing hydropower production.

This interaction requires some level of feedback between the WEAP generated hydropower and the energy model OSeMOSYS when designing the optimal energy adaptation plan. A two-cycle WEAP-OSeMOSYS feedback was chosen based on the trade-off of computer time and closeness to stable equilibrium. Figure 2.3 outlines the feedback loops employed in these models. The optimization tool is shown as a dashed line around the water model. In effect, the optimization tool runs the water model many times to search for a more resilient set of infrastructure capacities, with reference to a particular climate. The optimization tool provides an alternative investment profile for evaluation by the water and power pool, as shown in figure 2.1, but with a scenario-specific set of prices derived from the OSeMOSYS model, as opposed to the reference scenario prices. The performance of these new profiles can then be evaluated against the "no adaptation" estimates developed in chapter 5. As indicated in chapter 3, the computational complexity of the adaptation approach requires us to focus on adaptation to just six of the 121 climate futures. That means that the study team calculated sets of alternative *investments* only for the *six* representative climate futures, but then evaluated the *performance* of the altered infrastructure capacity profile *against all 121 climate futures*, to assess which of the six strategies might provide the greatest adaption gains across the full range of climate futures.

Figure 2.3 Schematic of the Perfect Foresight Adaptation Optimization Tool

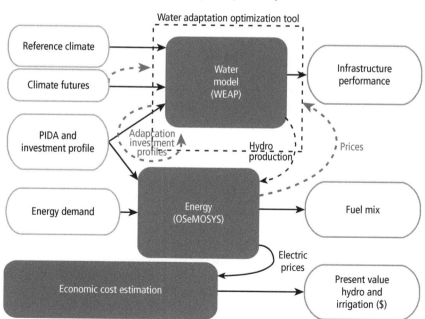

Note: OSeMOSYS = Open Source Energy Modeling System; PIDA = Program for Infrastructure Development in Africa; WEAP = Water Evaluation and Planning system.

Robust Adaptation

The goal of the robust adaptation analysis is to identify potential water and power infrastructure investment plans that perform well over a wide range of potential future climates—acknowledging that "well" can be defined in different ways, by different decision makers. This stage of the analysis recognizes that climate and other uncertainties are deep, in the sense that they cannot be confidently characterized by any single probability distribution. In addition, these uncertainties may not be resolved anytime soon. The robust adaptation analysis does not necessarily aim to provide a strict ordering of investment strategies, but rather to identify a few potentially robust strategies and to identify for decision makers the key trade-offs among the robust strategies.

Performance of Perfect Foresight Adaptations in Alternative Climates

As a first step in the robust adaptation analysis, the analysis calculates the performance of each of the perfect foresight adaptations (Case C) in each of the representative climate futures, including futures other than the one for which the adaptation was optimized. For instance, these calculations explore the implications of the case where decision makers invest expecting a wet future and are faced with a dry one instead, or vice versa.

To calculate these cases for a particular perfect foresight adaptation, the analysis team holds the irrigation and hydropower investment decisions unchanged and calculates the economic performance of those investments in each of the six representative climate futures. These investment decisions, while held constant, have benefit and cost implications, so the estimates are net present values. For irrigation, in each such calculation, the study team holds the area of irrigated crop choices and investments in on-farm efficiency unchanged from the perfect foresight case. For hydropower, in each such calculation, the analysis holds the irrigated conveyance efficiency, turbine capacity, and storage level unchanged from the perfect foresight case. In the language of the climate change adaptation literature, the investments in irrigation and hydropower infrastructure generally represent planned adaptations (which may or may not prove maladaptive).

Comparative Robustness of Perfect Foresight Adaptations (Case D)

To compare the robustness of the alternative investments generated by the perfect foresight adaptation analysis, the analysis calculates the regret of each such strategy in each representative climate future. The regret of a strategy in any future is the difference between its performance (net present value) and the performance of the best strategy in that future. A perfect foresight adaptation will have zero regret in the climate future for which it was optimized and nonzero regret in other futures. In particular, it is reasonable to expect that a perfect foresight adaptation for a wet future will have a relatively large regret in a dry future and vice versa.

Having calculated these regrets, the study team applies two decision criteria to identify robust strategies. First, the analysis reports the strategy that minimizes the maximum regret (mini-max regret criteria)—this reflects a risk-averse approach, which is focused on minimizing the regrets of the most extreme negative outcome, even if that extreme outcome is represented by only one or a very few climate futures. Second, the analysis reports the strategy that has small regret over a substantially large number of futures (a domain criteria), for example, 75 percent of the climate futures. In this case, a certain number of negative outcomes (the worst 25 percent) are excluded from the optimization problem.

Statistics and visualization of the database of the simulation model results can help decision makers identify the conditions in which proposed policies will not meet their goals and the trade-offs among alternative strategies. In general, robust decision-making (RDM) analyses do not provide a strict ranking of options, but rather help organize information for decision makers so that they can better weigh their choices. In particular, RDM analyses often highlight key trade-offs among alternative decision options that decision makers might consider. That is the approach adopted here. In this study, as is often the case, it proves useful to use robustness criteria that involve measures of regret, a comparative measure that tracks how well any particular strategy performs in a future state of the world, in relation to the best-performing strategy in that state of the world (Savage 1954).

As described elsewhere, RDM and probabilistic risk analyses generally give the same results when using similar assumptions (Lempert and Collins 2007; Lempert, Sriver, and Keller 2012). Under conditions of deep uncertainty, however, such as those that define climate change forecasting, RDM analyses can reduce the potential for disagreement among stakeholders who have different expectations about the future, increase understanding of the sensitivity of proposed plans to potentially stressing futures, and help yield strategies that are more robust against the uncertainties. See box 2.2 for more information on the impact of differing robustness criteria on decision making in this study, and online appendix F for more details on the RDM approach.

Water and Power System Modeling Tools

The hydrological and water balance model applied for the seven river basins is the WEAP model (www.weap21.org). WEAP is a globally available model developed by the Stockholm Environment Institute and improved over the course of more than 20 years. There are currently more than 10,000 registered users on the WEAP user forum, located in more than 170 countries.

BOX 2.2

Criteria Used for Robust Adaptations

This study makes use of a criterion called mini-max regret for choosing robust adaptation strategies, but this is not the only method for selecting robust adaptations. When decision makers are uncertain about the future, the mini-max regret criterion suggests calculating the worst-case regret for each strategy over the full range of plausible futures and choosing the strategy with the smallest worst-case regret. Because mini-max regret focuses on worst cases, it can sometimes suggest strategies very different from those that decision makers would choose if they focused on futures they regard as more likely.

Mini-max regret assumes a high level of risk aversion and no reliable probabilistic information. The expected utility criterion often used in economic analyses assumes risk neutrality and high-confidence probabilistic information. Other robustness criteria lie between these two extremes. In Track 1, we considered three alternatives: mini-max regret; a criterion that selects the strategy with the smallest 90th percentile regret; and a criterion that selects the strategy with the smallest 75th percentile regret. In the six basins for which we considered robust adaptations, the 75th and 90th percentile regret criteria suggest the same adaptation strategy as the most robust strategy. In five of the six basins, all three criteria suggest the same robust adaptation strategy. In one basin (Zambezi), there is a small difference between the strategies selected by the mini-max and 75th percentile criteria.

In Track 2, however, we considered three slightly more refined robustness criteria: mini-max regret; a criterion that selects the strategy with small regret over the largest number of futures; and a criterion that selects the strategy with small expected regret for a wide range of likelihoods. For most of the five projects considered, the three criteria suggest similar robust adaptations, but not in all cases. For example, in the Lower Fufu project, the mini-max regret criterion suggests the smallest diversion tunnel (with a maximum flow of 29 cubic meters per second [m^3/s]), but a design of 39 m^3/s has small regret over the largest number of future climate conditions, and a design of 31–33 m^3/s has small regret over the largest number of future climates excluding the extremely low flows. Thus, decision makers who are most concerned about very low-flow worst cases should consider a design with small tunnels (29 m^3/s). Decision makers who are less concerned with worst cases, and who consider all the futures equally likely, might consider large tunnels (39 m^3/s). Decision makers who are concerned with limiting their exposure to extreme dry futures, but who believe those futures to be relatively unlikely, might consider tunnel size between these extremes and, by coincidence, a capacity close to that which would be optimal based on historical climate.

The WEAP applications for the seven river basins integrate climate-driven routines for estimating streamflow and agricultural water demand in systems models designed to explore the impact of different management strategies and investments under a range of uncertainties for each basin. Each river basin model relies on historical and projected time-series of monthly climate data inputs (i.e., precipitation and minimum and maximum temperatures) to simulate the hydrologic response (i.e., rainfall-runoff, evapotranspiration, groundwater recharge, etc.) within the river basin and the water requirements for each of the main current and anticipated formal irrigation schemes located throughout the river basins. This approach allows for the consideration of how changes in climate impact the timing and magnitude of water available to support all the management objectives within the basin, including hydropower generation, urban water use, irrigation, navigation, fisheries, and environmental flows.

The hydropower representation in the WEAP model, applied at the basin level, is necessarily somewhat simplified. Hydropower output from WEAP is a time-series of total monthly energy. As a result, the WEAP model and basin analyses in general are not well suited for modeling the specific circumstances surrounding hydropower facilities that are constructed for peaking load purposes, rather than base load. In addition, it is difficult to conduct the basin-scale power pool modeling with an adequate representation of peaking load energy prices for peaking load facilities. This proved to be a particular concern for the Niger basin; further details are provided in box 2.3.

The WEAP applications for each of the seven river basins use the 0.5 by 0.5 degree gridded historical climate data from Princeton University (mentioned in chapter 3) to validate the model over the period from 1960 to 2005. Model validation criteria include estimates of natural streamflow, agricultural and domestic water usage, and reservoir storage and releases. These historical data were obtained from national- and/or basin-level databases that are typically maintained by national ministries and/or river basin commissions. Details of the WEAP model and applications to seven river basins can be found in online appendix C.

The power system model that was applied for the four power pools is implemented in an open source, transparent energy modeling system (OSeMOSYS) (Howells et al. 2011). The model extends and improves upon previous efforts in coverage of technologies, structure, and data. In particular, the analysis builds on the African Infrastructure Country Diagnostics (World Bank 2010), which provided special insights at the national level, and on the Program for Infrastructure Development in Africa (PIDA 2011), which provided an integrated regional outlook. Specific improvements include the following:

- The analysis features a higher techno-economic resolution, while building on the openness of the General Algebraic Modeling System environment used in the Africa Infrastructure Country Diagnostics.

BOX 2.3

Special Considerations for Modeling Peaking Hydropower Plants

In the standard Track 1 methodology, the approach applies a monthly simulation of hydropower production. The hydropower output from the Water Evaluation and Planning system results in a time series of total monthly energy production, which in turn is fed to the OSeMOSYS power pool model. OSeMOSYS takes the total monthly generation and distributes it to four time slices: peak and non-peak and weekdays and weekends, within the constraints of the maximum capacity of the facility. This approach is valid for raw energy generation and fits well within the OSeMOSYS economic optimization analysis. It does not, however, allow for consideration of expected higher energy prices in calculating the revenues for a facility designed for peaking load operation.

Further, in the perfect foresight adaptation analysis for Track 1, the study team employed an "average value" of energy generation. However, any economic or financial analysis at the monthly level with average costs is not valid for peaking plant and pumped storage facilities, where the range of prices for electricity generation between peak and non-peak can be four to five times. In general, the Track 1 approach, at the basin level, was not designed to assess particular facilities—this was left to Track 2. As long as the peaking plants in the Track 1 analysis have relatively small capacities, the overall degree of error introduced by this simplification will generally be small.

In one case, however, the simplified treatment of peaking plants proved to be a particular concern for a proposed 3,000 megawatts plant in the Niger basin, the Mambila facility in southeastern Nigeria. This new facility represents roughly 65 percent of the proposed new hydropower production, and was designed to provide peaking power to the Nigerian grid and West African Power Pool. As a result, the project team chose to conduct a sensitivity analysis on the perfect foresight results for the Niger basin. The results are presented in chapter 6.

- The model structure has been improved to achieve detailed representation of individual countries and subregions, at the monthly resolution needed to represent hydro variability in such an integrated assessment (Howells et al. 2013).

- Finally, planned infrastructure location, capacity, and performance data are taken from the latest available power pool studies and available databases (such as IRENA 2013a, 2013b; SNC.LAVALIN 2011; PLATTS 2013; and others). In the case of the Southern African Power Pool (SAPP), the largest in the region, the modeling is being undertaken in close collaboration with

SAPP staff members, who intend to use the results of the modeling for their own planning activities. Details are provided in online appendix D.

The technologies that are considered include existing as well as new power generation options. Future plans for technology installation are taken into account and split into three categories: committed, proposed, and generic. This breakdown offers multiple levels of flexibility and translates into the following types of technology building blocks within the model:

- Each identified hydropower project is represented by a specific technology.
- Technologies relating to committed projects are forced into operation on the planned year of installation at the relevant capacity level.
- Potential projects—available from their corresponding start-up dates—are left as optional: no forcing is used.
- Site-specific projects are populated with site-specific cost and performance data, derived mainly from International Renewable Energy Agency studies.
- Each technology category also has a generic option with generic cost and performance data.

To improve the model's representation of the role of decentralized power options, for which renewables can offer a significant cost advantage over fossil-based options, the power demand was split into three categories: industrial, urban, and rural electricity use. Each demand is provided through a dedicated energy chain. The energy chains include different capital costs for distribution line technologies, depending on the assumed remoteness of the demand, but also enable multiple generation options to be made available to each category of power demand.

Fossil and renewable technologies are envisaged in this work. The first enter the system through the use of domestic reserves and import options that are available for relevant countries. The second include all typical renewable fuels and are introduced through technologies that do not generally require any input. The existing grid is modeled with explicit representation of any corresponding transnational connections. As per production technologies, existing and committed transmission lines have fixed installation dates, while future identified options are made available for installation in certain scenarios.

Cross-border transmission lines play a fundamental role in distributing energy resources that are scattered unevenly among the countries in each power pool region. Some countries may be extremely rich in either fossil or renewable resources, giving those countries great potential for exporting electricity to less fortunate neighboring areas. Since the energy models investigate minimal overall system cost, the results of the investigatory scenarios with varying levels of interconnectedness show a clear correlation between higher levels of trade and lower cost of electricity. In other words, trade enhances resilience, but the base case runs assume only that signed and agreed transmission projects are incorporated. Other PIDA+ transmission investments that may be under consideration are not incorporated in the analysis.

In OSeMOSYS, these transmission lines are represented by technologies that link two parallel energy chains from two neighboring or "interconnected" countries. The technologies transfer electricity from one secondary level to the other and are set up as so-called "two-way" connectors: using two modes of operation, the same technology (with the same techno-economic parameters) can transfer energy in both directions during any time slice where active capacity for this technology exists.

Track 2 Analysis

The Track 2 analysis uses a variant of the same four-step process identified in table 2.1, but with a few modifications to align the approach with analysis of project-level considerations, and focuses specifically on engineering design modifications and, in some cases, financial risk management mechanisms at the project level. The five test projects generally consider a broader set of uncertainties than those in Track 1. For example, one of the test projects examines uncertainty in municipal water demand as a key interactive factor in the climate vulnerability of water infrastructure. Another test project examines the role of electricity prices as agreed in a power purchase agreement for hydropower output. The policy levers are specific to each case study, but focus on engineering design choices, such as dam height, storage, and turbine size. The metrics include firm yield (hydropower), safe yield (water supply), levelized cost of hydropower generation and water supply, and net present value of investment.

The scoping process includes defining a range of alternative designs, which include one that is appropriate for historical climate but also variations that are appropriate for wetter or drier climates (Step 1). Each design is evaluated for each of 145 climate projections (including 24 alternative historical trajectories). The analysis summarizes the design's strengths and weaknesses compared with other designs. The analysis then employs three alternative robustness criteria to suggest the most robust strategy. In general, the criteria give similar rankings that yield different information about the comparative strengths and weaknesses of the designs.

As with Track 1, the analysis does not aim to provide a definitive ranking of alternative designs, but rather aims to clarify the key trade-offs facing policy makers and suggest ways in which they might choose among the options available to them.

Notes

1. An important technical reality associated with linking the WEAP river basin models and the OSeMOSYS power pool models is that there is not a perfect overlap of modeling domains. Although the seven river basins represent a substantial portion of actual and potential hydropower generation potential in Africa, there are other sources of hydroelectricity in each of the four power pools beyond those represented in the WEAP models. These are generally small hydropower sources and represent a small portion of the overall generation capacity in the four power pools. The project team considered several options to address this concern and chose to make the assumption that all other hydropower potential represented in the OSeMOSYS power pool models varies according to some aggregate assessment of the variation in generation for hydropower projects that are represented in WEAP models of the basins linked to the power pool model. As a result, while these other hydropower sources are not explicitly modeled, their generation is dynamic with climate change in a manner that tracks the generation dynamics of the modeled hydropower generation for the power pool as a whole.

2. It is plausible that in much of Africa, consumers will not just accept a price increase to continue consuming the same quantity as before the dry climate shock. The adjustment will probably lead to substitution in the consumption basket of crops affected by declining production with either (a) other crops less affected by climate shocks or (b) imports of the same crops from overseas, to the extent that these have not been affected by the domestic climate shock. The larger the price elasticity of demand, the smaller will be the effect of omitting from the analysis the price effect on revenues.

3. In strictly economic terms, the trade-off does not seem to favor intensive irrigation development, despite the employment opportunities and the food security that such development might provide; their development benefits in economic terms are offset by the value lost in hydropower generation. The development of irrigation in this analysis has another important aspect: direct employment. Building and operating irrigation systems demands a lot of labor and thus creates job opportunities. Hydropower generation also produces direct jobs, of course, but except in the relatively short construction period, employment opportunities are limited to those with necessary skills (World Bank 2010).

References

FAO (Food and Agriculture Organization of the United Nations). 1998. "Crop Evapotranspiration: Guidelines for Computing Crop Water Requirements." FAO Irrigation and Drainage Paper 56. FAO, Rome. http://www.fao.org/docrep/x0490e/x0490e00.htm#Contents.

Howells, M., S. Hermann, M. Welsch, M. Bazilian, R. Segerstöm, T. Alfstad, D. Gielen, H. Rogner, G. Fischer, H. van Velthuizen, E. Wiberg, C. Young, A. Roehrl, A. Mueller, P. Steduto, and I. Ramma. 2013. "Integrated Analysis of Climate Change, Land-Use,

Energy and Water Strategies." *Nature-Climate Change* 3 (7): 621–26. doi:10.1038/
NCLIMATE1789.

Howells, M., H. Rogner, N. Strachan, C. Heaps, H. Huntington, S. Kypreos, A. Hughes,
S. Silveira, J. DeCarolis, M. Bazillian, and A. Roehrl. 2011. "OSeMOSYS: The Open
Source Energy Modeling System: An Introduction to Its Ethos, Structure and
Development." *Energy Policy* 39 (10): 5850–70. http://dx.doi.org/10.1016/j
.enpol.2011.06.033.

IRENA (International Renewable Energy Agency). 2013a. "Southern African Power
Pool: Planning and Prospects for Renewable Energy." IRENA, Abu Dhabi.

———. 2013b. "West African Power Pool: Planning and Prospects for Renewable
Energy." IRENA, Abu Dhabi.

Lempert, R. J., and M. Collins. 2007. "Managing the Risk of Uncertain Threshold
Responses: Comparison of Robust, Optimum, and Precautionary Approaches." *Risk
Analysis* 27 (4): 1009–26.

Lempert, R., R. L. Sriver, and K. Keller. 2012. "Characterizing Uncertain Sea Level Rise
Projections to Support Investment Decisions." California Energy Commission,
Sacramento, CA.

Nelson, G., M. W. Rosegrant, A. Palazzo, I. Gray, C. Ingersoll, R. Robertson, S. Tokgoz,
T. Zhu, T. B. Sulser, C. Ringler, S. Msangi, and L. You. 2010. *Food Security, Farming,
and Climate Change to 2050: Scenarios, Results, Policy Options*. Washington, DC:
International Food Policy Research Institute.

PIDA (Program for Infrastructure Development in Africa). 2011. "Study on Programme
for Infrastructure Development in Africa (PIDA) Phase III: PIDA Study Synthesis."
SOFRECO Led Consortium. African Union, Addis Ababa, Ethiopia.

PLATTS. 2013. UDI PLATTS World Electric Power Plants Database (WEPP). http://
www.platts.com/products/world-electric-power-plants-database.

Savage, L. J. 1954. *The Foundations of Statistics*. Mineola, NY: Dover Publications.

SNC.LAVALIN. 2011. *Regional Power System Master Plan and Grid Code Study—
Volume I* [Online]. Prepared for EAPP/EAC (Eastern Africa Power Pool/East Africa
Community). http://www.eac.int/energy/index.php?option=com_docman&
task=cat_view&gid=63&Itemid=70.

World Bank. 2010. *The Costs to Developing Countries of Adapting to Climate Change: New
Methods and Estimates*. Washington, DC: World Bank.

Chapter 3

Climate Change Projections in Africa

*Brent Boehlert, Kenneth M. Strzepek, David Groves,
Bruce Hewitson, and Chris Jack*

Figuring out how exactly infrastructure development should be modified to take climate change into account is difficult, because of the high degree of uncertainty in climate projections. First-generation analyses of adaptation have implicitly tended to adopt the assumption of "perfect foresight," entailing the ability of decision makers to predict whether a "dry" or a "wet" climate future would materialize, and thus to determine the appropriate adaptation response accordingly. However, climate change projections are highly uncertain. The disagreement among climate models is such that for several regions in Africa it is not even possible to determine whether rainfall will decrease or increase in the future.

Since no consensus has yet emerged in the climate science community on how to assign probabilities to alternative hydrological futures, a conventional method assuming a single or even a small set of climate futures cannot be utilized to plan investment under climate uncertainty. Instead, approaches have been suggested to identify "robust decisions," that is, those that perform well compared with the alternatives over a wide range of plausible futures. The first step toward the application of such an approach is to define the "uncertainty domain," that is, to define across the continent a range of climate projections that adequately captures uncertainty about climate processes (reflected in the wide range of general circulation models), as well as future greenhouse gas (GHG) emissions pathways. This chapter reviews the methods for developing such a range of climate futures, against which investment plans are tested.

Developing Climate Change Projections

There are at least four steps in virtually any projection of future climate:

1. *Characterize history.* This step involves choosing a representation of the historical climate, which is used to relate the projection to existing conditions.

2. *Characterize the principal climate change drivers.* This step requires choosing a GHG emissions pathway that represents a reasonable projection of the phenomenon believed to drive future climate change.

3. *Process the emissions data in a climate model.* This step involves using a general circulation model (GCM) (or models) with which to process the emissions projection to develop trajectories of climate indicators (such as temperature and precipitation).

4. *Relate the model projections to historical data.* This step relates the projections to historical information on the temporal and spatial variability of current climate, while also taking into account information from climate models about how these patterns could change in the future. In technical terms, this process involves spatially and temporally downscaling and bias-correcting the climate projections, relating the model results from the GCMs to the characterization of historical conditions, at the desired spatial and temporal resolution.

At each step of the process, there are choices and uncertainties. Although some consensus exists concerning what not to do in each of these steps, there are multiple valid alternatives for completing each step. As a result, many reasonable projections exist of future climate change for any location and time period, which could be used in impact and adaptation analysis. A key element of the current science that drives the methods applied here, however, is that climate scientists have not generally agreed about the relative likelihood of these multiple projections.

In light of this circumstance, the study team chose to employ climate information from emissions scenarios and climate models, as well as multiple bias correction and spatial downscaling techniques. Bias correction is a process that uses measured historical climate information to normalize the outputs from the models. This process effectively ensures that what we take from each climate model is a representation of the modeled differences the model implies between historical and future climate. Spatial downscaling is a process of enhancing the spatial resolution of the relatively crude spatial projections from climate models, through judicious use of historical information. Bias correction and spatial downscaling processes derive from the conclusion that it would be inappropriate to use the results of climate models directly; instead, it is better to use historical climate information to ground the results. Each of the approaches used for developing downscaled future climate projections is defensible scientifically and provides information on different possible realizations of future climates. Box 3.1 provides technical details on the procedures that are applied.

The result of this approach is 24 characterizations of the historical climate for Sub-Saharan Africa, which are necessary to provide a clear representation of natural variability in climate systems, and a total of 121 alternative

BOX 3.1

A Technical Summary of the Methods for Developing Climate Futures

The following types of data were used to develop climate sequences:

Historical climate sequences. The analysis uses data from the Terrestrial Hydrology Research Group at Princeton University, organized in a grid at 0.5 degree resolution (approximately 50 kilometers) covering Africa for the period 1948 to 2008. This data set merges what is currently one of the most comprehensive collections of daily observed records from the Global Historical Climatology Network with a number of re-analysis and satellite or satellite/station merged gridded data sets.

Downscaled global *climate projections* of future climate using the Bias Corrected Spatial Disaggregation (BCSD) method. The BCSD method is a development of pattern scaling, incorporating quantile mapping to account for general circulation model (GCM) biases in rainfall intensity distributions. The strengths of this method are that the projections show strong agreement with GCM projected changes on a large scale, and that the method produces a de-biased future projected time-series, which greatly eases the application to impact modeling, particularly hydrology.

Track 1 basin- and power pool–scale analyses use the results of *two classes of climate models*, which were supported as part of the two most recent assessments of the United Nations Intergovernmental Panel on Climate Change (IPCC): the Fourth (AR4) and Fifth (AR5) Assessments, published in 2007 and 2013, respectively. The AR4 provided data from 22 GCMs, which were evaluated across three emissions scenarios. Because not all models were deployed for all three emissions scenarios, the data yielded a total of 56 emissions-GCM combinations for our use. The results were processed with the BCSD method to produce a monthly time-transient time-series for a 50-year period representing 2001 to 2050 at a 0.5 by 0.5 degree resolution grid across Africa for rainfall and temperature.

The IPCC AR5 provided data from 23 GCMs, and the study team employed results for *two emissions pathways*, designated representative concentration pathway (RCP) 4.5 and RCP 8.5, corresponding to medium and high emissions scenarios, respectively. RCP 8.5 corresponds to the emissions pathway often emphasized in characterizations of the World Bank's recent report, "Turn Down the Heat: Why a 4°C Warmer World Must Be Avoided." Combining the GCMs and emissions scenarios yielded a total of 43 additional emissions-GCM combinations, also processed with the BCSD method.

An *additional 22 climate futures* (11 GCMs driven by the 4.5 and 8.5 RCP emissions pathways) were produced with an alternative downscaling technique, the Empirical-Statistical Downscaling Methods developed at the Climate Systems Analysis Group at the University of Cape Town. This method relies on different outputs from the GCMs in the downscaling process, focusing on the atmospheric pressure results, which are then related to precipitation outcomes, rather than using the precipitation outcomes from the GCMs directly.

(continued next page)

Box 3.1 (continued)

The BCSD method also yields a useful byproduct: 23 *simulated historical period baselines* developed from the AR5 suite of 23 GCMs and BCSD bias correction methodology. This set of simulated historical periods is used in the project to supplement the actual historical data, based on the Princeton baseline data, with the advantage that the historical baseline for the project from which the study team measured changes can be augmented by an alternative set of historical characterizations that may reflect a broader view of historical "without climate change" conditions. Although it may seem counterintuitive to generate multiple "histories" of climate, the rationale is that the sequence of wet and dry years in the actual history of African climate represents only one manifestation of natural variability in climate. By using a set of simulated histories that have the same distribution of wet and dry periods, but random variations in sequences, we enhance the likelihood that, when we ground our projections in history, we do not limit the projections to a single sequence of wet and dry periods, but instead include a richer set of possibilities for future climate sequences.

representations of the climate future, each of which can be used to estimate the impacts of climate change on infrastructure performance and the adaptation options that can be deployed to respond to those impacts. The approach utilized in the present report to develop climate projections complements the one adopted by the Turn Down the Heat series of reports, as discussed in detail in box 3.2.

Temperature and Precipitation Results by Basin

The results of our broad characterization of climate futures indicate that a wide range of outcomes are possible in each of the study basins. Figure 3.1, panel a, shows the temperature results for the Volta basin for the historical period and the projections through 2100 (the results are similar for other basins). As indicated in the figure, all temperature forecasts show increases over time, but the magnitude of the increase for any single projected trajectory can differ markedly, with estimates for the end of the century ranging from a 1-degree to a 7-degree increase. Estimates for the highest GHG emissions scenario, the Coupled Model Intercomparison Project—Reference Concentration Pathway 8.5 (CMIP5-RCP8.5), show the highest degree of warming over time.

Figure 3.1, panel b, shows comparable results for precipitation forecasts, for the Volta basin. In the case of precipitation, however, the overall results show almost no discernable trend, even when the end of the century is considered; instead the results are marked by very high year-to-year and cross-GCM

BOX 3.2

Comparison of Climate Projections in This Study with Those in the Turn Down the Heat Reports

The projections used in this study reflect the broad base of climate science that underlies the last two assessment reports of the Intergovernmental Panel on Climate Change (IPCC)—the fourth and fifth assessment reports, commonly referred to as AR4 and AR5. A recent World Bank–supported effort, the "Turn Down the Heat" (TDH) series of reports, relies on the most recent IPCC climate science base, the AR5, as well. The TDH reports use the same AR5 emissions scenarios (the representative concentration pathways, or RCPs) and the same set of AR5 General Circulation Models (GCMs) as this report. Differences between the climate projections presented in TDH and this report stem mainly from three sources:

- *How the general circulation models are used.* Rather than using the GCM results as they are provided by the IPCC, the TDH reports present ensemble results by running a climate model ensemble of 600 realizations for each greenhouse gas (GHG) emissions scenario. In the simulations, each ensemble member is driven by a different set of climate model parameters that define the climate system response, including parameters determining climate sensitivity, carbon cycle characteristics, and many others. Some filtering is then conducted, so that randomly drawn parameter sets that do not allow the climate model to reproduce a set of observed climate variables over the past centuries (within certain tolerable "accuracy" levels) are filtered out and not used for the projections, leaving the 600 realizations that are assumed to have adequate predictive skill. The current study, by contrast, uses the results of GCMs directly, and then conducts downscaling and bias correction calculations for each of the individual emissions-GCM scenario combinations. In short, TDH tends to focus on aggregate ensemble results; this study tends to focus on ensemble members.

- *How the emissions scenarios are used.* TDH relies mostly on two RCPs—3.0 and 8.5. RCP 3.0 is a mitigation scenario, while RCP 8.5 is largely acknowledged to be a non-mitigation scenario. This study also uses RCP 8.5, but for the mitigation scenario, it relies on RCP 4.5, which reflects recent thinking that the failure to date to reach an international climate agreement on GHG emissions reductions makes the realization of RCP 3.0 less likely. This study also uses other emissions projections from the older AR4.

- *How the time period of interest is defined.* For most of their results, the TDH reports present outcomes for mid-century, centered on 2050, and for end-century, reflecting the period 2080–2100. The use of "eras" to present mid-century and end-century results is appropriate for illustrating the temperature, precipitation, sea level rise, and extreme event endpoints that are the focus of TDH. But results

(continued next page)

Box 3.1 (continued)

for eras typically are not used as inputs in biophysical and economic models of climate impacts. This study focuses on the period from the present (effectively 2010) to mid-century, 2050, which is relevant for decision making for new infrastructure in the next 15–20 years. A monthly time-series of climate projections is used to drive the biophysical and economic models of the water resource and power pool systems.

The cumulative effect of these differences is that the climate scenarios used in this study span a broader range of discrete climate model and emissions scenario outcomes than TDH, which is appropriate for the purposes of the current study, which focuses on methods for addressing uncertainty in climate futures.

Figure 3.1 Illustration of Model Variation for Temperature and Precipitation Futures, Volta Basin

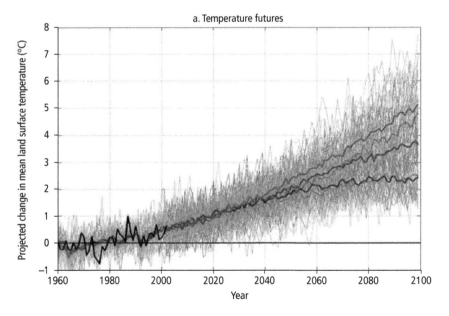

(continued next page)

Figure 3.1 (continued)

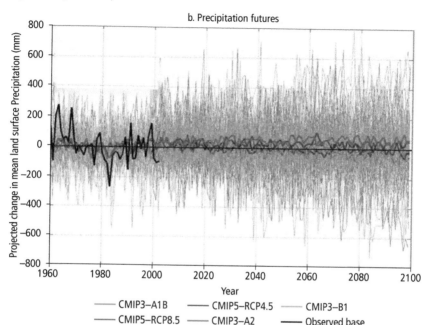

Note: CMIP3 corresponds to the IPCC Fourth Assessment General Circulation Model (GCM) results; CMIP5 corresponds to the IPCC Fifth Assessment GCM results. CMIP = Coupled Model Inter-comparison Project; RCP = representative concentration pathways. The observed base reflects only the measured (Princeton) data set base.

variability. In addition, the higher emissions scenarios (CMIP5-RCP8.5) tend to show more wetting than the lower emissions scenarios. Further, the results shown are for the entire 21st century, while in this study our time horizon extends only to 2050.

The results can also be summarized by comparing the degree of aridity, which is a combination of changes in temperature and humidity. An index that is commonly used to measure aridity is the Climate Moisture Index (CMI). Results for the CMI for the seven focus basins (with the Nile divided into two major sub-basins) are presented in figure 3.2. The results indicate that each of the basins exhibits a particular historical pattern, with the Congo generally the wettest and the Eastern Nile the driest in Sub-Saharan Africa, and the projections showing both drier and wetter futures than the historical climate. The results support the point that the range of alternative climate futures cannot be readily summarized as either wetter or drier than the historical climate. This finding reinforces the need to consider a framework such as robust decision

Figure 3.2 Comparison of Aridity for the Study River Basins
(Climate Moisture Index)

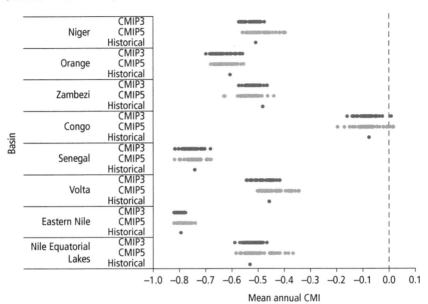

Note: The Climate Moisture Index (CMI) is a measure of aridity that combines the effect of rainfall and temperature projections—the effect of higher temperature is to increase evaporation. The index values vary between −1 and +1, with lower values representing more arid conditions. A CMI value greater than zero indicates that, for that basin, rainfall rates are greater than potential evapotranspiration rates. CMI is often a good proxy indicator for measures such as river runoff and irrigation demands. CMIP3 corresponds to the IPCC Fourth Assessment general circulation model (GCM) results; CMIP5 corresponds to IPCC Fifth Assessment GCM results. Historical reflects the measured (Princeton) data set.

making (RDM) (described in more detail in chapter 4), which allows the analyst to consider a broad range of future outcomes when making infrastructure planning decisions. With uncertainty in the pattern of future climate, the possibility to over- or under-design climate-sensitive infrastructure is considerable; a wiser course of action would be to consider the outcomes of alternative infrastructure plans across the broadest feasible set of futures. The range of historical and projected outcomes also reinforces the need to consider multi-basin connectivity as an adaptation option—for example, countries in wetter basins, such as the Congo may be well-positioned to provide hydropower to countries in other, drier basins.

Another important conclusion from figure 3.2 is that the range of uncertainty in climate projections has tended to increase over time.

The earlier-generation CMIP3 results, in blue, show a tighter distribution than the latest CMIP5 results. The most recent advances in climate science, therefore, do not seem to narrow uncertainty, but reflect an increase in uncertainty. This conclusion provides another important rationale for adopting the RDM methods used in this study in planning climate-sensitive infrastructure deployment.

The full range of 121 alternative representations of the climate future can be used in many parts of the analysis, but as the calculations of the adaptation response become more complex in our analytical chain, it becomes necessary to narrow the number of scenarios that can be reflected. The CMI results illustrated in figure 3.2 can be readily calculated for all the climate futures and all seven river basins. The results provide a good basis for selecting representative scenarios for more in-depth analysis (as is done in chapter 6), while preserving the variability in results that is indicative of each basin, particularly for precipitation forecasts.

Another way to view the climate scenarios is shown in figures 3.3, 3.4, and 3.5, presented for the three basins of the Southern African Power Pool (Congo, Orange, and Zambezi), the three basins of the West African Power Pool (Niger, Senegal, and Volta), and the Nile basin. Here the horizontal axis is the average annual temperature for the basin and the vertical axis is the average annual precipitation in millimeters. The X's shown in a cluster toward the bottom of the graphs represent the historical climate, with red X's corresponding to the modeled CMIP5 baseline and the blue X corresponding to the measured Princeton historical baseline. The orange and green symbols indicate the CMIP3 and CMIP5 projections, respectively, and the various symbols in the legend provide an indication of the emissions scenario.

As is clear from these figures the historical temperatures are lower than all the temperature futures, but the historical precipitations generally sit in the middle of the range of the precipitation futures. The newer CMIP5 projections tend to represent the more extreme temperature and precipitation projections (at the top and right in the figures, respectively), particularly those for the "high-end" emissions scenario, RCP 8.5, shown as orange diamonds.

Looking across basins, the relative positions of the historical results to the left or right of the cluster of future climate projections give some indication of whether the study team can expect a largely drier or largely wetter future in these basins. For example, the Nile and Niger basin results suggest more wetter than drier futures, while the Zambezi suggests there is some possibility of a much drier basin. As noted above, however, there is no way to assign probabilities to the 121 climate futures, so the study team should not interpret likelihoods from these results. Rather, the study team can think of the climate

Figure 3.3 Climate Futures in 2050 for the Congo, Orange, and Zambezi Basins

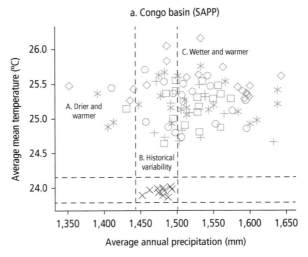

a. Congo basin (SAPP)

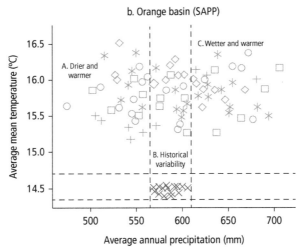

b. Orange basin (SAPP)

(continued next page)

Figure 3.3 (continued)

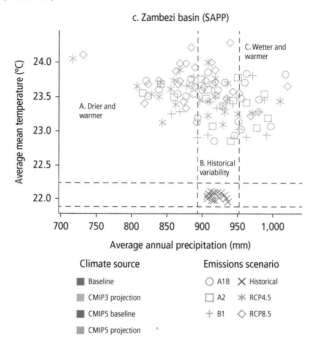

c. Zambezi basin (SAPP)

Climate source	Emissions scenario
■ Baseline	○ A1B ✕ Historical
▨ CMIP3 projection	☐ A2 ✳ RCP4.5
■ CMIP5 baseline	+ B1 ◇ RCP8.5
▨ CMIP5 projection	·

Note: mm = millimeters.
1. CMIP3 corresponds to IPCC Fourth Assessment General Circulation Model (GCM) results; CMIP5 corresponds to IPCC Fifth Assessment GCM results. Baseline reflects the measured (Princeton) data set, and the CMIP5 baseline reflects the 23 simulated histories (see box 3.1) for more details.
2. The A quadrant refers to climate scenarios that are on average drier and wetter than the historical record; the B quadrant refers to scenarios that are warmer than the historical record, but within the historical range of variation of precipitation (as proxied by climate models); and the C quadrant comprises scenarios that are warmer and wetter than the historical record.

futures as indicative of a range of possibilities for each basin that are supported by the best current climate science from the Intergovernmental Panel on Climate Change.

The climate futures therefore provide an initially plausible space for thinking about the range of possible climate impacts (as outlined in chapter 5) and the range of climate futures that can be considered in future adaptation planning and design (as presented in chapters 6 and 7). In addition, it is important to note that "drier" in water resource planning is a combination of temperature and precipitation, as higher temperatures lead to higher evaporation from surface waters, higher evapotranspiration from plants, and as a result, lower runoff in

Figure 3.4 Climate Futures in 2050 for the Niger, Senegal, and Volta Basins

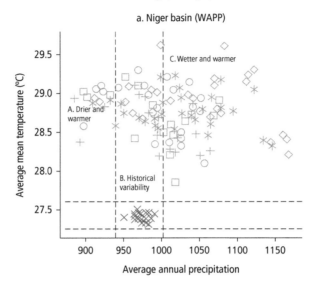

a. Niger basin (WAPP)

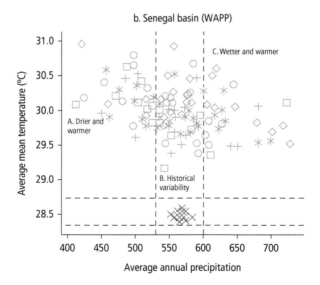

b. Senegal basin (WAPP)

(continued next page)

Figure 3.4 (continued)

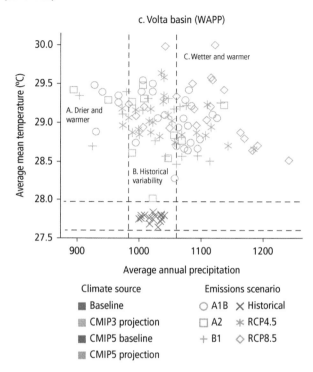

c. Volta basin (WAPP)

Climate source
- ■ Baseline
- ▨ CMIP3 projection
- ■ CMIP5 baseline
- ▨ CMIP5 projection

Emissions scenario
- ○ A1B   ✕ Historical
- □ A2   ✳ RCP4.5
- + B1   ◇ RCP8.5

Notes:
1. CMIP3 corresponds to IPCC Fourth Assessment General Circulation Model (GCM) results; CMIP5 corresponds to IPCC Fifth Assessment GCM results. Baseline reflects the measured (Princeton) data set, and the CMIP5 baseline reflects the 23 simulated histories (see box 3.1) for more details.
2. The A quadrant refers to climate scenarios that are on average drier and wetter than the historical record; the B quadrant refers to scenarios that are warmer than the historical record, but within the historical range of variation of precipitation (as proxied by climate models); and the C quadrant comprises scenarios that are warmer and wetter than the historical record.

rivers, all else being equal. Finally, these figures provide a sense of the annual mean values, but the impact and adaptation results presented in later chapters make use of the monthly results for each basin and sub-basin the study team considered. The monthly patterns of temperature and especially precipitation vary considerably across Sub-Saharan Africa, and the more refined temporal patterns have the most influence on impacts in the agriculture and hydropower sectors. For example, a scenario that appears "wet" in annual terms can still incorporate a monthly forecast that suggests a hotter, drier agricultural season, which would suggest climate change impacts that are negative for agriculture, rather than positive.

Figure 3.5 Climate Futures in 2050 for the Nile Basin

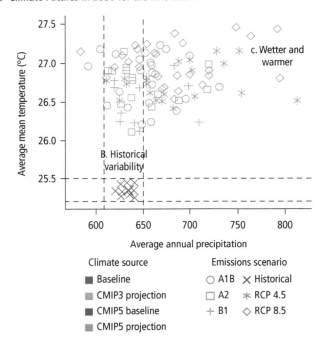

Notes:
1. CMIP3 corresponds to IPCC Fourth Assessment General Circulation Model (GCM) results. CMIP5 corresponds to IPCC Fifth Assessment GCM results; Baseline reflects the measured (Princeton) data set, and the CMIP5 baseline reflects the 23 simulated histories (see box 3.1) for more details.
2. The A quadrant refers to climate scenarios that are on average drier and wetter than the historical record; the B quadrant refers to scenarios that are warmer than the historical record, but within the historical range of variation of precipitation (as proxied by climate models); and the C quadrant scenarios that are warmer and wetter than the historical record.

For some components of the Track 1 analysis, in particular to support our adaptation analyses, the study team needed to focus on fewer representative climate futures. A small set of futures was chosen to provide a good sample of the range of consequences implied by the full range of the 121 climate futures used in the climate change vulnerability and impact analysis. Given the computational and analyst time involved with each perfect foresight calculation, the study team was able to conduct six such calculations for each of the seven river basins. The process for identifying an appropriate representative set of six climate futures, from among the 121 alternative climate futures in our ensemble, is described in online appendix E.[1] In summary, the process uses the CMI, which combines precipitation and temperature and is reasonably well correlated with the hydropower and irrigation impacts expected from each climate projection, to find a set of consistently wet and dry climate futures across the seven basins under analysis. Figures 3.6, 3.7, and 3.8 show how the six representative futures compare with the range of all 121 climate futures on the CMI relative to the historical baseline (Climate 0), and how the representative futures are named for the basin-scale analyses throughout the remainder of this report.

For the adaptation analysis, the study team sought to retain in the six futures used for more detailed analysis a few scenarios where the outcomes are inversely correlated across basins. For example, in some climate futures, dry conditions for some periods of time in the Southern African basins correspond with wet periods in the West African basins. A careful examination of figures 3.6, 3.7, and 3.8 indicates that Climates 39 and 90 fit this category—they

Figure 3.6 Representative Climate Futures for West African Basins
(Climate Moisture Index values)

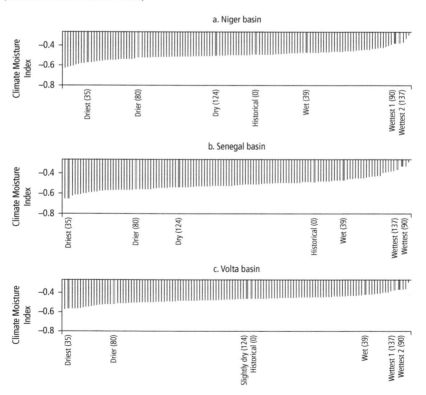

Note: The numbers in parentheses are reference numbers for futures.

Figure 3.7 Representative Climate Futures for Southern African Basins
(Climate Moisture Index values)

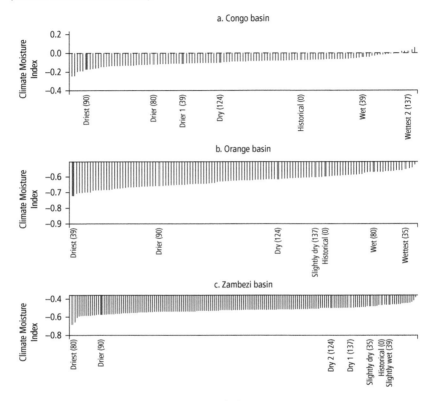

Note: The numbers in parentheses are reference numbers for futures.

Figure 3.8 Representative Climate Futures for the Nile Basin
(Climate Moisture Index values)

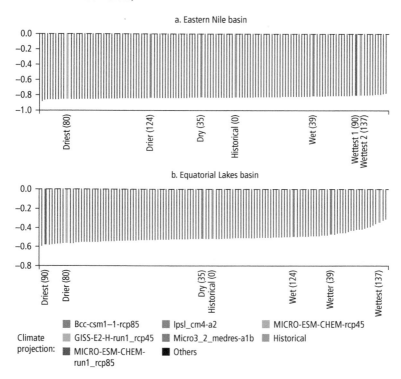

Note: The numbers in parentheses are reference numbers for futures.

are wetter than the historical climate in some basins and drier than the historical climate in others. Analysis of these scenarios provides an opportunity to test whether enhanced interconnectivity of these two regions of Africa could in fact contribute to enhanced collective climate resilience, through interregional trade of hydropower.

Note

1. Appendix E is available online at https://openknowledge.worldbank .org/handle/10986/21875.

Chapter 4

Reference Investment Scenario

Annette Huber-Lee, Stephanie Galaitsi, Casey Brown,
Abdulkarim Seid, Denis Hughes, and Brian Joyce

Infrastructure Expansion beyond PIDA: PIDA+

For each river basin and power pool focus, the starting point of analysis is the definition of a development baseline, that is, a plausible set of development targets against which to gauge climate change effects, as well as the merits of alternative adaptation options. The targets are expressed in physical terms (e.g., megawatt hours (MWh) per year of power and millions of hectares equipped for irrigation) and in monetary terms (e.g., present value [PV] of the revenues from irrigation or power projects). The development baseline reflects continent-wide priorities, as expressed in the Program for Infrastructure Development in Africa (PIDA) (PIDA 2011), as well as subregional and national investment plans that were reviewed and subsequently vetted specifically for inclusion in this study (e.g., World Bank 2010). The baseline is therefore labeled PIDA+. The basis for defining PIDA+ includes official documents from national (governments) and regional public bodies (river basin organizations) (see online appendix A for a full list of sources).[1] The inclusion of projects in PIDA+ has no implications for the World Bank's endorsement of the projects, and no attempt has been made to evaluate the technical or economic merits of the projects included in PIDA+ or to assess the realism of their implementation timeline. PIDA+ represents the study team's best effort to characterize regional and national priorities and goals for hydropower and irrigation expansion over the 2015 to 2030 time horizon.

Methodology

The first step in defining a reference case, or infrastructure baseline, as described in chapter 1, is to incorporate projects in the PIDA program. The projects included are in the hydropower and irrigation sectors, in the seven basins in the geographic scope of the study, that are slated to be developed between 2015 and 2030, the temporal scope of infrastructure enhancement in the study. Although the study team did not consider projects that might be slated to begin after 2030, the study estimates climate change effects on all projects through 2050.

The next step is to augment PIDA with additional projects that might be reflected in the regional or national infrastructure master plans within the same sector, geographic, and temporal scope. A total of 62 institutions that have some authority and responsibility for infrastructure and climate change in Africa were identified and contacted by the project team. In total, 99 contacts with staff working in these institutions were established, and information from these sources was combined with information available online, published literature, and other readily available sources. As a result of this process, a total of 300 investment projects related to hydropower schemes, agriculture and irrigation, overall water resources, and water supply were identified (see de Condappa and Barron 2013). The projects were grouped by basin and country and, as much as possible, their project status, budget, and investor and donor were indicated. The projects were then added to the list of PIDA projects to constitute the PIDA+ scenario. Only projects with insufficient information on their important design parameters, capacities, and timing to implementation were omitted.

The original PIDA did not include irrigation. To address irrigation invest-ments, the project team undertook an additional process to identify the location and extent of existing irrigation schemes, and then identified specific projects through local contacts to generate the future investment profile. Both elements— existing and planned infrastructure—are important to the modeling conducted here. All climate-sensitive infrastructure needed to be included in the water sys-tem modeling, as it represents an important existing and future demand on water supply for each basin (that is, irrigation demand increases with higher aridity) that needs to be reflected in an analysis of the impacts of climate change. The informa-tion on irrigated areas in the seven basins is scattered. Therefore, three sources of information were examined, each representative of a particular spatial scale:

1. At the scale of the African continent: general and international databases
2. At the basin scale: documents developed by basin organizations or direct outreach to basin organizations
3. At the national scale: national water ministries or projects of the riparian countries.

The sources for the African continent are from the Food and Agriculture Organization (FAO) and are summarized in table 4.1. The reports from FAO have the advantage of presenting the data for African countries in a relatively uniform pattern, as the information in AQUASTAT is collected with uniform methods at the national level.

Table 4.1 References for Irrigation Information at the African Continent Scale

Reference	Type of information
FAO 2005	AQUASTAT profile for each country
FAO 2013	Subnational irrigation
Siebert et al. 2007	Global Map of Irrigation Areas Version 4.0.1

Google Earth was also used to locate as precisely as possible existing irrigation schemes and to check that the schemes are still in operation. Individual irrigation schemes were identified whenever possible; otherwise, the irrigation schemes were agglomerated as spatial clusters. Future irrigation projects were derived from de Condappa and Barron (2013) based on review of national-level agriculture master plans, published river basin organization documents, and consultations with selected river basin organizations. See online appendix A for more details.

Results

The detailed results of this process are included in tabular form in online appendix A. Summary results are presented in table 4.2. The table provides a summary of the full range of PIDA+ capacities, for existing hydropower and irrigation areas, for each of the seven basins. In the *reference scenario* of investment, hydropower capacity in the seven basins considered in this study could increase by almost six times, irrigation capacity by more than 60 percent, and storage capacity by more than 80 percent.

The economic performance of the reference scenario is summarized in table 4.3, for the new investments reflected in the PIDA+ scenario. The results indicate that the present value (PV) of the revenue stream from these investments over the time horizon of this study is substantial, in excess of US$600 billion, based on the hydropower and crop price assumptions outlined in chapter 2. The Niger basin accounts for roughly one-third of this total, and 97 percent of the Niger PV is from irrigation investments throughout the basin (the increase of nearly 1.8 million hectares indicated in table 4.2). In the Congo, Nile, and Zambezi basins, the PV is largely attributed to hydropower investments. The scope of the work in the Orange basin includes only the Upper Orange, lying upstream of the confluence with the Vaal River. In that sub-basin of the Orange, there are no major new hydropower investments, and no irrigation investments in the PIDA+ scenario. The new investment in the Lesotho highlands area, the Polihali Dam project, is instead addressed in the Track 2 analysis; see chapter 7 for more details.

Table 4.2 Summary of Existing and Planned Hydropower and Irrigation Capacity in PIDA+

Basin	Existing hydropower capacity (MW)	Future additional hydropower capacity (MW)	Existing irrigation capacity (ha)	Future additional irrigation capacity (ha)	Existing storage capacity (MCM)	Future additional storage capacity (MCM)
Congo	1,858	44,402	20,282	No new areas	40,000	100,000
Niger	1,994	4,667	738,011	1,791,457	43,763	85,786
Nile	2,542	21,392	6,220,270	772,350	234,751	241,816
Orange	680	48[a]	66,530	No new areas	13,918	2,322[a]
Senegal	200	877	75,460	255,327	11,890	14,200
Volta	1,673	484	27,909	177,389	167,341	52,689
Zambezi	4,827	8,204	244,542	668,542	139,557	37,547
TOTAL	13,774	80,074	7,765,688	4,854,870	651,220	534,360
		(+581%)		(+63%)		(+82%)

Note: ha = hectares; MCM = million cubic meters; MW = megawatts.
a. This relatively small additional hydropower in the Upper Orange basin, associated with the development of the Lesotho highlands water projects, is excluded from the Track 1 analyses at the basin scale, but its design is addressed in the Polihali test project in Track 2. See chapter 7 for more details.

Table 4.3 Estimated Present Value of Revenues for PIDA+ Infrastructure Expansion, 2015–50 *(US$, billions)*

Basin	PV of hydro revenues	PV of irrigation revenues	Total
Congo	151.9	—	151.9
Niger	6.6	188.8	195.3
Nile	54.0	48.5	102.2
Eastern Nile	30.3	43.5	73.8
Equatorial Lakes	23.7	5.0	28.7
Senegal	4.5	38.1	42.6
Volta	2.6	25.6	28.2
Zambezi	65.1	20.6	85.8
All basins	282.1	321.6	603.8

Note: PV = present value; — = not applicable.

The estimated costs to implement the PIDA+ investments for the water and power sector, which are summarized in table 4.4, are substantially less than the projected revenues summarized in table 4.3. However, the costs in table 4.3 do not include the costs for Inga 3 or the Grand Inga investment, so the Congo basin's hydropower benefits should be largely excluded when making this comparison (see box 4.1 for more details on the Grand Inga and Inga 3 investment modeling assumptions). Total investment costs for the seven basins are approximately US$73 billion, with the largest portions in the Niger, Nile, and Zambezi basins.

Table 4.4 **Estimated Present Value of Investment Costs for PIDA+ Infrastructure Expansion, 2015–50**
(US$, billions)

Basin	PV of hydropower investment costs	PV of irrigation investment costs	Total
Congo	1.84[a]	0.00	1.84
Niger	6.41	8.28	14.69
Nile	34.14	2.52	36.66
Senegal	1.91	0.89	2.80
Volta	1.46	1.98	3.44
Zambezi	10.81	2.88	13.69
All basins	56.57	16.55	73.12

Note: PV = present value.
a. Excludes investment costs in Congo basin for Inga 3 and Grand Inga; see text and box 4.1 for explanation.

The handling of the reference scenario for Inga 3 and Grand Inga, two long-planned projects that, if implemented, could significantly alter the role of hydropower in Southern Africa and for the continent as a whole, is outlined in box 4.1. As noted in the box, the existing high flow in the Congo basin at the Inga site, and the expectation (confirmed by the vulnerability analysis described in chapter 5) that climate change is unlikely to reduce that flow except in a few extreme future climate forecasts, suggest a lack of climate sensitivity for the portions of the Grand Inga project that are likely to be constructed during the study period. As a result, the Inga 3 and Grand Inga projects are excluded from the climate adaptation analyses.

Of the roughly 80,000 megawatts (MW) of future additional hydropower capacity envisioned in PIDA+, approximately 10,500 MW is already under construction, effectively limiting the options for adaptation envisioned in this study. Most of the activity under construction is accounted for by the 6,000 MW Grand Ethiopian Renaissance Dam in Ethiopia. It is much more difficult to assess the extent to which irrigation capacity may be under construction or still in the planning stages.

For many of the projects still in the planning stages and not yet under construction, significant amounts of resources have already been invested in feasibility and environmental impact studies, as well as groundwork to set the stage for the projects. Although some projects have stalled, many of the hydropower plants included in the reference scenario have been under consideration for years or even decades. Although it is unclear whether such deliberations will make their eventual construction inevitable, it is reasonable to expect that the projects will move forward with the support of local constituencies, even if at this stage they are not yet fully funded or designed.

BOX 4.1

The Inga 3 and Grand Inga Hydropower Projects in the Congo Basin

Hydropower could be the mainstay of the Congo basin and the energy future of the Democratic Republic of Congo. The Democratic Republic of Congo has more than 100 gigawatts of hydropower potential, roughly five times the current installed capacity of all of Africa. Because the Congo basin covers areas in both hemispheres, the seasonality of hydropower generation in the Democratic Republic of Congo is much lower than elsewhere.

The largest single potential hydropower facility in Africa is Inga Falls, in the western portion of the Congo basin. Already some of this resource has been exploited—the Inga 1 hydropower plant was commissioned in 1972, and Inga 2 was added in 1982. Inga 1 and 2 have a combined installed generation capacity of 1,775 megawatts (MW). Both plants are currently under rehabilitation. The Program for Infrastructure Development in Africa also includes new installations—Inga 3 and Grand Inga, which are included in the scope of this study.

Inga Falls on the Congo River has unique hydroelectric potential and plans. A recent study recommended staged development of the Inga site to match the growth in demand in the Democratic Republic of Congo and other African countries and phased investments over time. Each project would represent an increment of 6,000 to 7,000 MW that could be built in five to seven years. The phased approach has been adopted by the government of the Democratic Republic of Congo and donors as a realistic approach to develop Inga's potential, and that approach is also adopted in this study. The assumptions used in this study are summarized in table B4.1.1.

The Inga 3 and Grand Inga plants are proposed plants, so they are included in all the aggregations of new plant performance throughout this report, for the Congo basin and Sub-Saharan Africa. Preliminary analyses, however, suggested that the abundance of water in the Congo basin, the low sensitivity of the Grand Inga resource to climate change, and the high likelihood that the full Grand Inga potential would not be reached before the sunset of the study horizon led the study team to conclude that Inga 3 and Grand Inga should be excluded from the adaptation analyses. Therefore, the reservoir and turbine capacities at the Inga site are left fixed in all the adaptation and robustness analyses conducted in this report.

Table B4.1.1 Summary of Assumptions

Project phase	Capacity (MW)	Projected year of completion
Inga 3	4,500	2023
Grand Inga	39,000	Five stages at 7-year intervals following implementation of Inga 3

Note

1. Appendix A is available online at https://openknowledge.worldbank.org /handle/10986/21875.

References

de Condappa, Deveraj, and Jennie Barron. 2013. "Assessment of Existing and Planned Irrigated Areas in the Congo, Niger, Nile, Orange, Senegal, Volta and Zambezi River Basins." Stockholm Environment Institute.

FAO (Food and Agriculture Organization). 2005. *Irrigation in Africa in Figures. AQUASTAT Survey – 2005.* FAO Water Reports 29. FAO, Rome, Italy. ftp://ftp.fao.org /agl/aglw/docs/wr29_eng_including_countries.pdf.

———. 2013. AQUASTAT. FAO, Rome, Italy. http://www.fao.org/nr/water/aquastat /main/index.stm.

PIDA (Program for Infrastructure Development in Africa). 2011. Study on the Programme for Infrastructure Development in Africa (PIDA) Phase III: PIDA Study Synthesis. SOFRECO Led Consortium.

Siebert, S., P. Döll, S. Feick, J. Hoogeveen, and K. Frenken. 2007. *Global Map of Irrigation Areas Version 4.0.1.* Johann Wolfgang Goethe University, Frankfurt am Main, Germany/FAO, Rome, Italy. http://www.fao.org/nr/water/aquastat/irrigationmap /index10.stm.

World Bank. 2010. "The Zambezi River Basin: A Multi-Sector Investment Opportunity Analysis (MSIOA)." Water Resources Management, Africa Region, World Bank, Washington, DC. http://documents.worldbank.org/curated/en/2010/06/13236172 /zambezi-river-basin-multi-sector-investment-opportunities-analysis-vol-1-4-summary -report.

Chapter 5

Impacts of Climate Change on Infrastructure Performance

Mark Howells, Brent Boehlert, Brian Joyce, Oliver Broad, Vignesh Sridharan, David Groves, Kenneth M. Strzepek, and Robert Lempert

Basin-Scale Performance of Infrastructure Relative to Overall Performance Targets

The first output from the climate change analyses described in chapter 2 is an assessment of infrastructure performance across multiple climate futures, relative to the reference case performance, that is, relative to performance for historical climate conditions. The results are presented in figure 5.1 for the three basins in the Southern African Power Pool (SAPP)—Congo, Orange, and Zambezi—and in figures 5.2 and 5.3, for the West African Power Pool (WAPP) and Nile basins. The vertical axis provides an assessment of irrigation sector performance, in units of percentage change in unmet irrigation water demand across the basin. Unmet irrigation demand is the difference between the amount of water demanded by plants in each climate (e.g., higher temperatures imply higher demand because of increased evapotranspiration; higher precipitation implies lower demand for irrigation because plant requirements are met from rainfall) and the amount of water that the Water Evaluation and Planning system water balance tool indicates is available for irrigation. The horizontal axis shows hydropower sector performance in electricity generation. For irrigation and hydropower, performance is measured cumulatively from 2015 to 2050. The reference lines for 0 percent correspond to the reference case of historical climate infrastructure performance in each basin. The circles in the graph represent the outcome in these two dimensions for a single climate future for each basin. For example, in figure 5.1, there are blue circles for Congo, green for Orange, and red for Zambezi.

The results in figure 5.1 show that under the driest scenarios, in the lower left corner, hydropower generation could decline by more than 60 percent, and

Figure 5.1 Infrastructure Performance under Climate Change for SAPP Basins: Existing and Planned Infrastructure, 2015–50

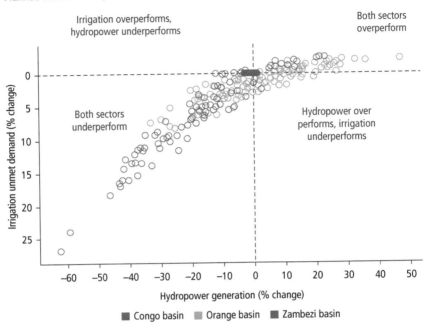

unmet irrigation demand could decline by more than 25 percent in the Zambezi basin. The benefits of wetter scenarios in the Zambezi basin, in the upper right corner, suggest an increase of up to 25 percent in hydropower production and a few percent in irrigation water provision. The results for the Orange basin are more balanced, with hydropower production outcomes clustering in the ±20 percent range, and unmet irrigation demand of no more than 10 percent. The results for the Congo basin show much less sensitivity to climate. This already wet basin could see hydropower reduced by up to 15 percent in one climate future and 10 percent in one other climate future, but for the vast majority of the other almost 120 climate futures, the results are within a few percentage points of that in the Congo reference case. Certainly, the results vary dramatically by basin, but overall climate change could be an important factor in water and power infrastructure performance in the SAPP.

The results for WAPP, in figure 5.2, show a high relative climate sensitivity for infrastructure in the Volta basin for hydropower and irrigation, and somewhat lower climate sensitivity in the Senegal basin (although with a skew toward drier scenarios and underperformance) and Niger basin. In figure 5.3 for the Nile basin, there is a high degree of climate sensitivity for the Eastern Nile and

Figure 5.2 Infrastructure Performance under Climate Change for WAPP Basins: Existing and Planned Infrastructure, 2015–50

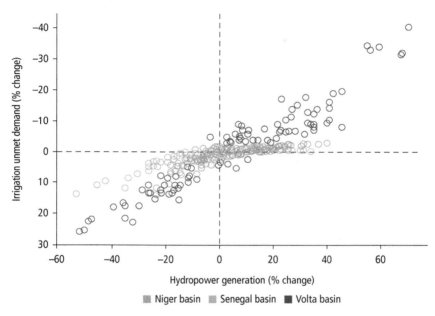

Figure 5.3 Infrastructure Performance under Climate Change for the Nile Basin: Existing and Planned Infrastructure, 2015–50

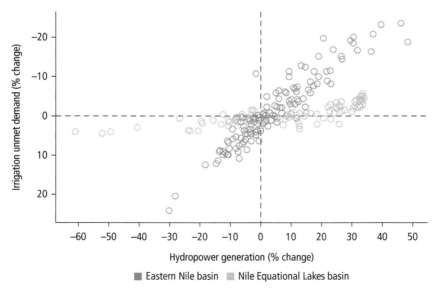

Equatorial Lakes sub-basins for hydropower and high sensitivity for irrigation in the Eastern Nile, but low sensitivity for irrigation in the mostly rainfed agriculture of the Equatorial Lakes sub-basin.[1]

Economic Costs of Ignoring Climate Change

Estimating economic impacts involves putting a value on the infrastructure performance shortfalls or windfalls that result from the full range of plausible climate futures. The prices used for hydropower revenues reflect market adjustments in the power pool to respond to underperformance or overperformance of hydropower relative to the historical case. In other words, the estimates account for the most basic, autonomous, and reactive market adaptations to climate impacts, in which power planners would react to changes in hydropower by adjusting the fuel mix for electric power (mainly by turning on or off fossil resources). Prices for irrigation infrastructure underperformance or overperformance are based on fixed cropping patterns (at historical levels) and a fixed price forecast, as described in chapter 2.

The resulting economic impacts of infrastructure performance are illustrated in figure 5.4 for SAPP, showing the percentage change in PV revenues,

Figure 5.4 Economic Impacts of Climate Change for SAPP Basins, Absent Adaptation

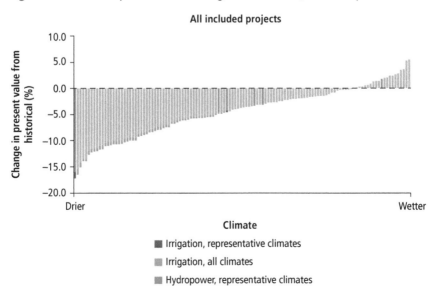

discounted at 3 percent, relative to that in the historical case for all facilities, current and new investments, in all three SAPP basins (Congo, Orange, and Zambezi). Each bar represents the results of a single climate future, with the orange portion of the bar showing the hydropower value component and the blue portion showing the irrigation value component. The bars are arranged from left to right in order of the overall economic impact, negative to positive, of each climate future. The results range from a decline in PV of 18 percent to an increase of just under 6 percent, and are dominated by hydropower value for the Zambezi and Congo basins, where irrigation infrastructure investments are a much smaller portion of the total than in other basins. In absolute terms, the total PV varies between US$230 billion and US$290 billion, with US$200 billion to US$260 billion accounted for by assistance from the new Program for Infrastructure Development in Africa plus irrigation investment (PIDA+), including the performance of Inga 3 and portions of the Grand Inga project built during this study's time frame. The Inga investments account for roughly half the present value revenues presented in figure 5.4. In addition, more than three-quarters of the climate scenarios examined show a negative outcome relative to historical performance in SAPP—confirming that SAPP investments may be highly vulnerable to climate change impacts, absent adaptation. For additional information on the Upper Orange basin, see box 5.1.

<hr>

BOX 5.1

<hr>

Impacts of Climate Change in the Upper Orange Basin

As outlined in chapter 4, the scope of the study in the Orange basin includes only the Upper Orange, lying upstream of the confluence with the Vaal River. In that sub-basin of the Orange, there are no major new hydropower investments and no new irrigation investments in the PIDA+ scenario. This scope for the Orange in the study is consistent with input received from the Orange-Senqu River Basin Authority during a July 2013 project workshop in Maseru, Lesotho. The new investment in the Lesotho highlands area, the Polihali dam project, is addressed in the Track 2 analysis (see chapter 7 for more details). As a result, the adaptation analysis for the Upper Orange focuses on the Polihali project.

Climate change impacts for the Upper Orange basin are significant for the current irrigation and hydropower investments in this sub-basin. Figure B5.1.1 indicates the range of present value (PV) of infrastructure performance across the 121 climate futures, for the period 2015 to 2050, at a 3 percent discount rate. As indicated, the PV varies from US$2.3 billion to US$4.1 billion for the worst and best climate futures, respectively, compared with a roughly US$3 billon PV under historical climate. Roughly two-thirds of the climate futures indicate infrastructure performance in excess of that

(continued next page)

Box 5.1 (continued)

Figure B5.1.1 Economic Impacts of Climate Change for Current Investments in SAPP Basins, Absent Adaptation

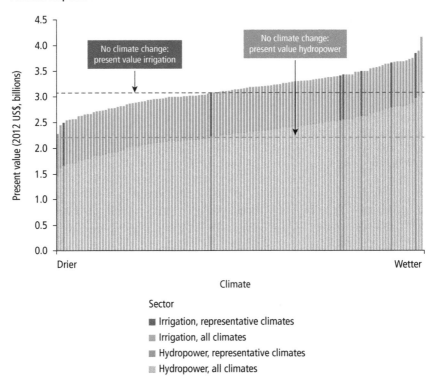

Sector
- Irrigation, representative climates
- Irrigation, all climates
- Hydropower, representative climates
- Hydropower, all climates

for the historical climate, which is consistent with most climate forecasts for wetter future conditions in this higher elevation portion of southeast Africa.

The variation of the irrigation component is smaller—from US$0.83 billion to US$0.88 billion across the changed climate futures, compared with US$0.87 billion in the historical climate—compared with the variation in the hydropower component—from US$1.4 billion to US$3.3 billion, compared with US$2.1 billion for the historical climate. These variations suggest a greater vulnerability, and climate opportunity, for hydropower in this basin.

Results for the SAPP and other basins presented in this chapter rely on the base case 3 percent discount rate assumption. It is important to note that the discount rate chosen has a substantial effect on the PV of the impacts of climate change. For example, for new investments in the SAPP basins, the PV of infrastructure revenues ranges from US$200 billion to US$260 billion with the default 3 percent discount rate, but it more than doubles for a 0 percent discount rate, is roughly 60 percent lower with a 7 percent discount rate, and is more than 75 percent lower with a 10 percent discount rate. The effect on adaptation choices is much less sensitive, although for energy infrastructure lower discount rates tend to result in a higher share of hydropower in electricity projections, while higher discount rates tend to result in a higher share of fossil energy.

Similar results for the three WAPP basins (Niger, Senegal, and Volta) are provided in figure 5.5. Considering all the WAPP basins and all the infrastructure, current and newly deployed as part of PIDA+, the projection for climate futures is wetter than for the SAPP basins. As a result, the economic impact of climate change for the WAPP basins varies from a decline of about 13 percent to an increase of nearly 15 percent or, in absolute terms, from US$275 billion to US$360 billion, relative to the reference case total of about US$315 billion. There are more outcomes with positive than negative results relative to the historical case. Irrigation investments are a more important component of the

Figure 5.5 Economic Impacts of Climate Change for WAPP Basins, Absent Adaptation

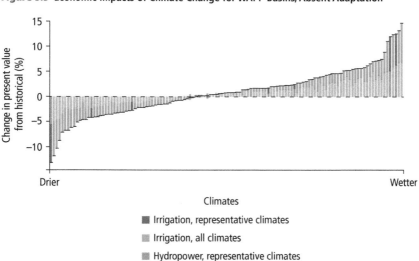

Figure 5.6 Economic Implications of Climate Change for the Nile Basin, Absent Adaptation

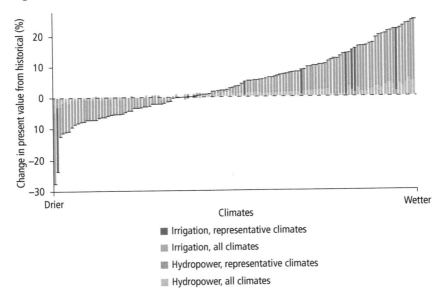

new PIDA+ investments for WAPP than for SAPP. Overall, however, the PIDA+ plus investments in WAPP are about as sensitive to climate change as the SAPP investments.

For the Nile basin, in figure 5.6, the economic impact of climate change absent adaptation varies from a decline of 28 percent to an increase of 23 percent or, in absolute terms, from about US$460 billion to about US$790 billion, relative to the reference case total of about US$630 billion. There are more outcomes with positive than negative results relative to the historical case, and irrigation clearly dominates the PV estimates. Considering all investments, current and new, the PV is dominated by the large existing irrigation presence in the Eastern Nile sub-basin, as indicated by the abundance of blue relative to orange portions of the bars. If only the new PIDA+ investments are considered, however, PV is roughly balanced between new hydropower and new irrigation investments. Overall, the water and power infrastructure in the Nile basin shows more sensitivity to climate change than other groups of basins in the study—and this sensitivity holds for current and new investments in the PIDA+ reference scenario.

Another way to look at these results is presented in figure 5.7 for the seven basins. In the figure, the box-and-whisker plots show all climate outcomes for each basin, with the extreme values indicated at the top and bottom of each column by horizontal lines, and the interquartile range (from the 25th percentile

Figure 5.7 Economic Impacts of Climate Change for All Basins, New Infrastructure, Absent Adaptation, in Present Value, with 3 Percent Discount Rate, 2015–50

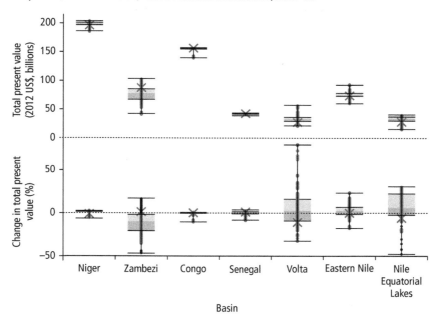

Note: The blue x represents the performance for the historical climate. The edges of the boxes indicate the 75th and 25th percentile performance; the edges of the whiskers show the 95th and 5th percentile performance; and the line that separates the light shading from dark shading marks the 50th percentile (median) performance.

to the 75th percentile, or the middle half of all the outcomes) represented by the gray box in the center of the image in each column. The blue X represents performance for historical scenarios. In absolute PV terms, in the top panel of the graph, the Niger basin investments have the highest PV, but the Zambezi investments are the most sensitive to climate change, showing a wide variation. The Volta and Eastern Nile basins are also sensitive in absolute terms. In percentage terms, in the lower panel of the graph, the Volta, Nile Equatorial Lakes, Zambezi, and Eastern Nile basins are the most sensitive to climate change, in that order.

Figures 5.8 and 5.9 present the economic impact results for hydropower and irrigation as separate categories. The results indicate that the Congo basin has the highest revenue potential from hydropower, but it is not very sensitive to climate change, in an absolute or relative sense. The Niger, Senegal, and Volta basins all have low revenue potential from hydropower, but the Volta's hydropower in particular is quite sensitive to climate change. The Zambezi, Eastern Nile, and Nile Equatorial Lakes basins' hydropower has substantial PV and

Figure 5.8 Economic Impacts of Climate Change for All Basins, New Hydropower Infrastructure, Absent Adaptation, in Present Value, with 3 Percent Discount Rate, 2015–50

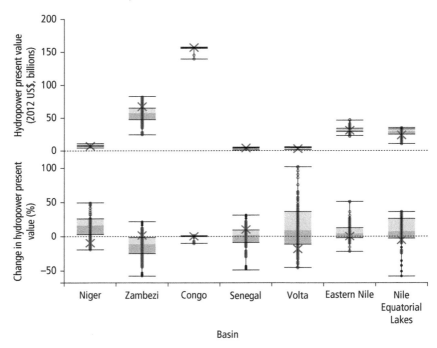

Note: The blue x represents the performance for the historical climate. The edges of the boxes indicate the 75th and 25th percentile performance; the edges of the whiskers show the 95th and 5th percentile performance; and the line that separates the light shading from dark shading marks the 50th percentile (median) performance.

shows clear sensitivity to climate change. For irrigation, the sensitivity of the Volta-irrigated areas is striking, but overall there is more at stake in an absolute sense in the Niger basin, albeit with a lower sensitivity to climate.

Table 5.1 provides a summary of the climate change analyses across all the basins. With no climate change, new infrastructure investments have the potential to generate more than US$600 billion in revenues over the period 2015–50 for the seven basins (first column of the table). With climate change, there is potential for almost US$60 billion in losses relative to the reference no-climate-change scenario and almost US$60 billion in "windfall" gains from climate change. Although these estimates are made with a no-adaptation assumption, the windfall may require some action to realize those revenues. For example, power purchase agreements could be restructured and/or investments could be made to ensure newly available hydropower generation or that irrigated crops can be brought to market at reasonable prices. The potential

Figure 5.9 Economic Impacts of Climate Change for All Basins, New Irrigation Infrastructure, Absent Adaptation, in Present Value, with 3 Percent Discount Rate, 2015–50

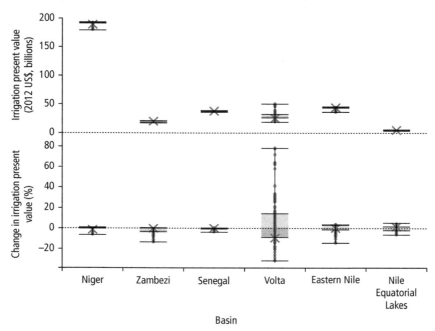

Note: The blue x represents the performance for the historical climate. The edges of the boxes indicate the 75th and 25th percentile performance; the edges of the whiskers show the 95th and 5th percentile performance; and the line that separates the light shading from dark shading marks the 50th percentile (median) performance.

costs of inaction, shown in the fourth column, are greatest in the Zambezi basin, with cumulative costs as much as US$45.0 billion in the driest scenarios. Losses could also be large in the Nile (US$26.8 billion) and Congo (US$16.6 billion) basins.

Power Pool Results: Fuel Mix and the Cost of Energy Provision

The integration of the water and energy models yields outputs in two categories: electric energy prices and fuel mix. The key mechanism by which climate change affects these outputs is hydroelectric facility performance. In wet climate futures, hydroelectric facilities generate larger amounts of electric power without any additional investment, which in turn allows hydro to replace certain other fossil-based electricity dispatch, and also reduces overall prices. The Open Source Energy Modeling System can generate these outputs at the power pool (multiple basins and countries) and country levels; both are reported here.

Table 5.1 Present Value of Revenues of Planned Hydropower and Irrigation Expansion, 2015–50
(US$, billions)

Basin	No climate change	Lowest PV (worst scenario)	Highest PV (best scenario)	Max reduction due to CC (worst scenario)	Max gain due to CC (best scenario)
Congo	156.2	139.6	157.1	−16.6	0.9
Niger	195.3	186.2	203.4	−9.1	8.1
Eastern Nile	73.8	60.3	92.0	−13.5	18.3
Nile Equatorial Lakes	28.7	15.4	40.2	−13.3	11.5
Orange	—	—	—	—	—
Senegal	42.6	38.7	43.4	−3.8	0.9
Volta	28.2	21.2	56.8	−7.1	28.6
Zambezi	87.5	42.5	103.2	−45.0	15.7
All basins	612.3	545.3	658.4	−67.0	46.1

Note: The all basins sum is not a simple sum of the worst case climate future in each basin, but reflects the single worst or best climate future as it affects all basins across all of Sub-Saharan Africa. As a result, the totals in the last four columns of the table are not sums of the basin-by-basin results. CC = climate change; PV = present value; — = not available.

A key summary statistic derived from the cost of power, however, is the PV of consumer expenditure on electricity, which is presented in table 5.2 for SAPP, WAPP, and the Eastern Africa Power Pool (EAPP), for selected countries—one sensitive to climate shocks and one less sensitive to climate shocks, primarily owing to dependence on hydropower. As the table indicates, dry scenarios raise prices and consumer expenditures in all power pools and all countries, but less so in countries such as South Africa and Nigeria, which have large fossil "backstop" options, than in countries such as Malawi and Mali, which are generally more reliant on climate-sensitive hydropower.

In general, the results in table 5.2 suggest that dry scenarios have a larger effect on consumer prices and that this effect is much more pronounced in SAPP than in the other power pools. This result is largely because of two factors in SAPP: transmission limitations and the relatively high percentage of hydropower in most parts of SAPP (outside South Africa). In wet scenarios, although it might be expected that a windfall of hydropower would lower prices significantly, the power pool optimization suggests that the windfall is not realized if significant effort is not expended to overcome transmission constraints. However, where transmission is not a constraint and hydropower shares are high, in countries such as Malawi and Tanzania, the hydropower windfall is reflected by significant declines in prices (by 9 and 5 percent, respectively).

Table 5.2 Present Value of Consumer Expenditure on Electricity, 2015–50
(US$, billions)

Power pool and country	No climate change	Driest scenario	Wettest scenario
Southern African Power Pool			
South Africa	1,214.47	1,769.49 (+46%)	1232.86 (+1.5%)
Malawi	6.27	19.54 (+212%)	5.72 (−9%)
Total	1,449.03	2,133.86 (+47%)	1448.37 (< 1%)
West African Power Pool			
Mali	18.41	22.16 (+20%)	17.72 (−4%)
Nigeria	683.73	691.49 (+1%)	677.40 (−1%)
Total	1,120.19	1,155.45 (+3%)	1089.24 (−3%)
Eastern Africa Power Pool			
Tanzania	66.46	81.78 (+23%)	63.16 (−5%)
Egypt, Arab Rep.	1,716.04	1,732.03 (+1%)	1711.62 (< 1%)
Total	2,344.44	2,417.32 (+3%)	2302.03 (−2%)

Figure 5.10 presents similar data for all countries in SAPP, WAPP, and EAPP. Countries to the left of the total (for the power pool–level effect) show greater sensitivity to the extremes of climate change in consumer expenditure for electricity, in part because they are small countries, but also in cases where there is a high dependence on hydropower. Countries to the right of the total are more resilient, although almost always because of the presence of fossil fuel backstop options, which in turn have implications for greenhouse gas emissions. The scale of change across the three power pools is also instructive—countries and the power pool as a whole in SAPP are more vulnerable to climate change extremes than are their counterparts in EAPP and WAPP. These "no-adaptation" results reflect the autonomous energy market response to changes in generation productivity associated with climate change; adaptation options are explored in chapter 6.

Figure 5.11 illustrates graphically the cost of electric power and fuel mix results at the power pool level for SAPP for wet and dry scenarios. Consistent with expectations, estimated costs are higher in the dry than wet scenario, and the total share of hydropower generation (the blue bars in the figure) is higher in the wet scenario, displacing fossil sources.

The effects on fuel mix are more pronounced at the country level than at the power pool level. At the power pool level, the ability to optimize dispatch across a wide portfolio of generation facilities tends to dampen the effect of climate change, but at the country level this portfolio effect is diminished.

Figure 5.10 Relative Vulnerability of Consumer Expenditures on Electricity to Climate Extremes, 2015–50

(Percent of no-climate-change expenditure)

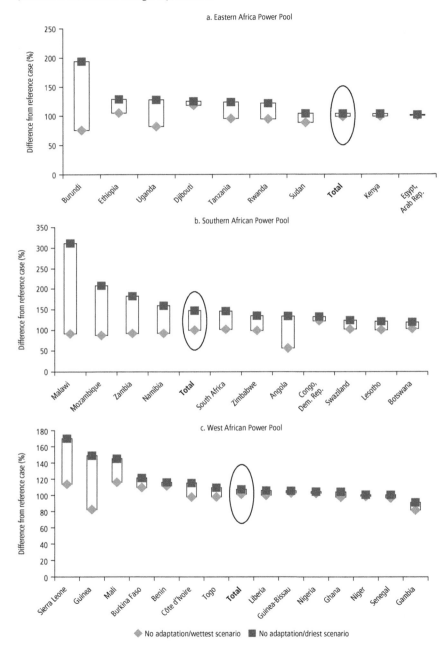

◆ No adaptation/wettest scenario   ■ No adaptation/driest scenario

Figure 5.11 Cost of Electric Power and Fuel Mix for SAPP, 2010–50

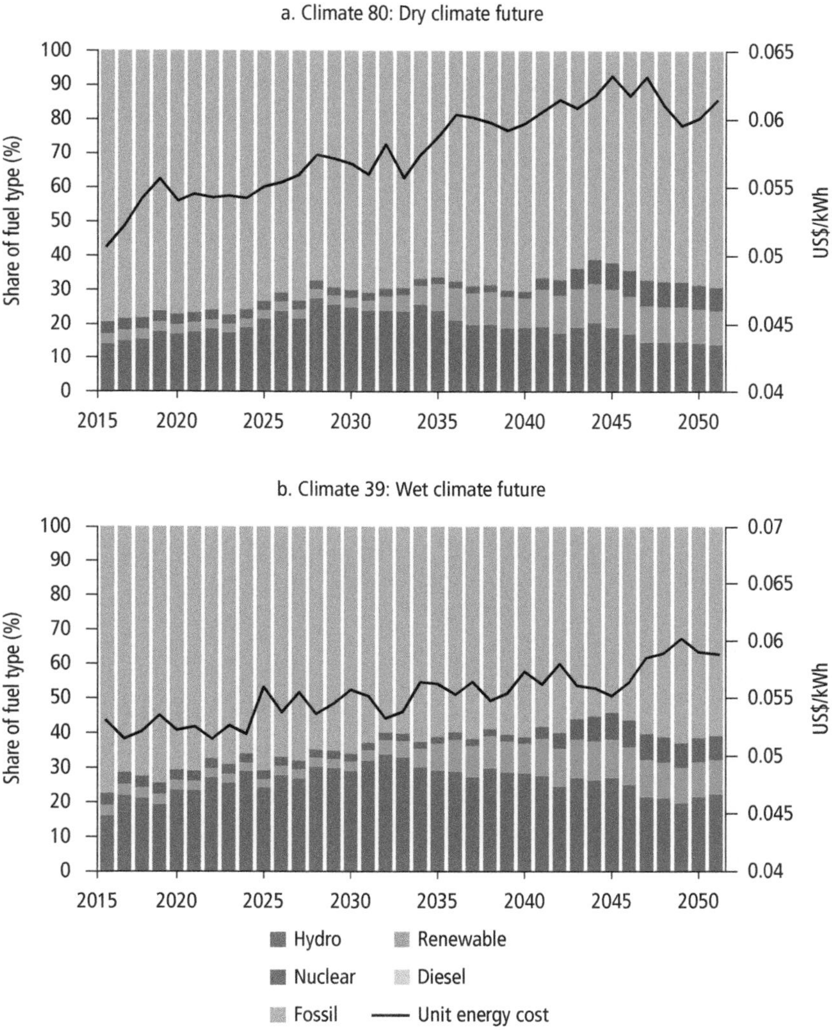

a. Climate 80: Dry climate future

b. Climate 39: Wet climate future

Hydro   Renewable

Nuclear   Diesel

Fossil   —— Unit energy cost

Note: The left y-axis is the percentage share of the electricity supply.

An example is given in figure 5.12 for Mozambique, a country where there is significant hydropower potential and several PIDA+ projects scheduled for investment during the study period, as well as an emerging fossil-based generation capacity. As shown in the figure, in the dry and wet scenarios, hydropower generation dominates in the early part of the study period and

Figure 5.12 Projected Fuel Mix for Mozambique under Climate Change, 2010–50

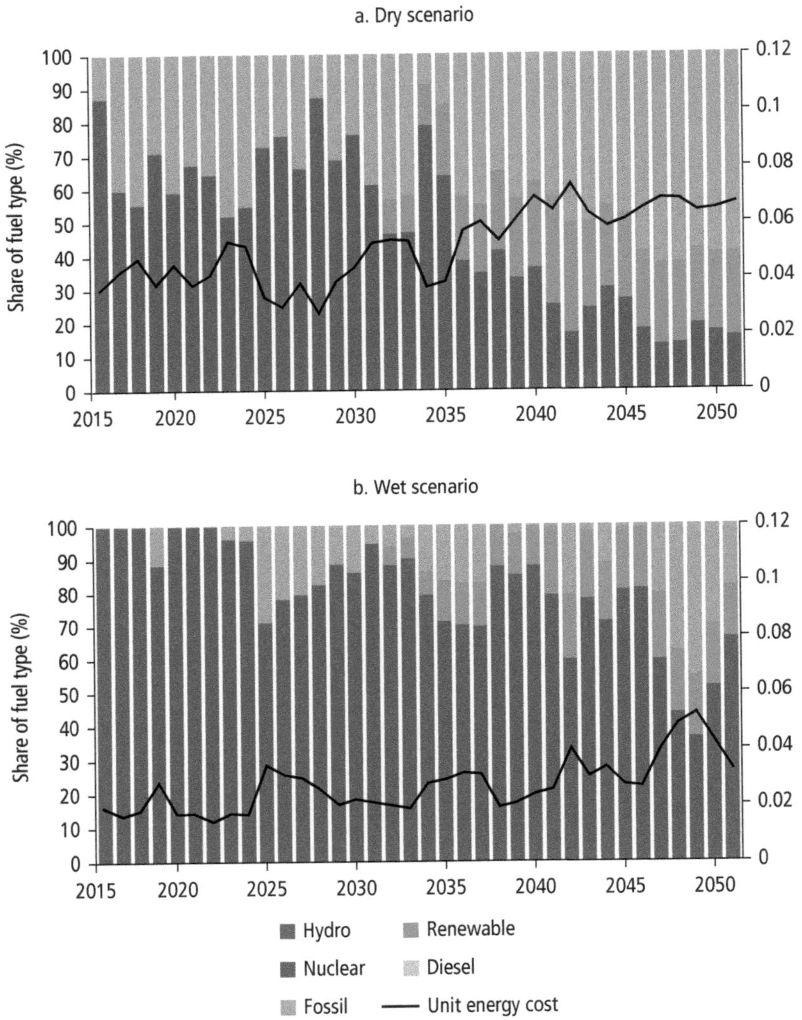

a. Dry scenario

b. Wet scenario

Legend: Hydro, Renewable, Nuclear, Diesel, Fossil, Unit energy cost

Note: The left y-axis is the percentage share of the electricity supply.

begins to be displaced by fossil generation starting in 2015. In the wet scenario, this displacement is largely reversed by 2020, while in the dry scenario fossil resources continue to expand through this period. By the end of the period, the need to meet electricity demand growth throughout the region requires an expansion of fossil resources, but in the wet scenario the hydro share is much higher than in the dry scenario, displacing fossil resources but also some higher-cost renewables.

Impacts on Agricultural Imports

Shortfalls in irrigated production, as described in the previous sections, could increase the demand for food imports. All basins have a baseline historical climate level of food imports, as indicated in the first column of table 5.3. In dry years, the need for imports increases; in addition, import prices are generally higher than the prices for domestic production. The crop price projections used in the analysis (Nelson et al. 2010) suggest that import prices on average are about 40 percent higher than prices for domestic production, for the crops expected to be grown in the newly irrigated areas in the study. As a result, production shortfalls that are made up by imports imply a substantial price premium.

The last two columns of table 5.3 outline the range of changes in imports, priced at the International Food Policy Research Institute's world market prices, for the worst and best climates. As expected, dry climate futures imply a substantial increase in import needs, which is especially acute in the Eastern Nile and Niger basins. More favorable climates imply a decreased need for imports, with very large reductions in import needs in the Eastern Nile and Niger, across all basins. Note that these analyses only indicate needs for imports implied by shortfalls on current and newly irrigated land—production on rainfed areas is not considered in the analysis, but could be substantial. For example, the generally arid Eastern Nile basin has a large percentage of irrigated production (one reason the estimates are so high for this basin), while the higher precipitation in the Nile Equatorial Lakes basin means it has a much higher allocation of rainfed production and low irrigated production in all scenarios. The clear implication is that climate change has important impacts on the demand for imports, with consequent effects on consumers associated with the expected higher prices for imported food production.

Table 5.3 Present Value of Agricultural Import Needs, 2015–50
(US$, billions)

Basin	No climate change	Worst climate	Best climate
Congo	0.00	0.00	0.00
Niger	7.62	20.43	2.20
Eastern Nile	100.30	383.96	6.01
Nile Equatorial Lakes	0.46	0.98	0.15
Senegal	0.10	2.09	0.07
Volta	46.91	58.11	10.65
Zambezi	0.56	4.82	0.18

Note

1. These sub-basins correspond to the division of the Nile Basin Initiative into two coordinated but independent subprograms. The Eastern Nile sub-basin includes the lower part of the Nile basin in the Arab Republic of Egypt, parts of Sudan and South Sudan, and the highland areas of the basin in Ethiopia. The Equatorial Lakes region includes portions of the Nile basin in Burundi, Kenya, Rwanda, Tanzania, and Uganda, as well as the western parts of Sudan, and South Sudan and a small portion of the Democratic Republic of Congo. For more information, see http://www.nilebasin.org/.

Reference

Nelson, G., M. W. Rosegrant, A. Palazzo, I. Gray, C. Ingersoll, R. Robertson, S. Tokgoz, T. Zhu, T. B. Sulser, C. Ringler, S. Msangi, and L. You. 2010. "Food Security, Farming, and Climate Change to 2050: Scenarios, Results, Policy Options." International Food Policy Research Institute, Washington, DC.

Chapter 6

Adaptation to Climate Change in Infrastructure Planning

*Robert Lempert, Brent Boehlert, David Groves,
James E. Neumann, Kenneth M. Strzepek, Oliver Broad,
Vignesh Sridharan, and Raffaello Cervigni*

Basin-Scale Analysis Overview: Scope and Value of Adaptation

As outlined in chapter 5, climate change has the potential to put water and power infrastructure performance at risk. In most basins, there is a significant chance the infrastructure will underperform as a result of a drier than expected climate. Changing infrastructure configurations and capacities, however, informed by knowledge of the range of future climate outcomes, has the potential to improve that performance. Even in forecasts for wetter conditions, there is potential for adaptation to improve outcomes by adjusting infrastructure capacities to match future climate projections. In this chapter, we present the results of our analysis on the substantial value of considering climate change when planning major climate-sensitive water sector infrastructure investments.

Figure 6.1 summarizes the flow of the analysis. In chapter 5, the Program for Infrastructure Development in Africa plus irrigation investment (PIDA+) infrastructure for each basin was evaluated across the 121 climate futures developed in chapter 3. The results show that the costs of inaction could be as high as US$60 billion in lost revenues.

In this chapter, the analysis first generates a set of potential adaptive responses by calculating the perfect foresight (PF) adaptation in each basin for each of the six representative climate futures identified in chapter 3. These PF adaptations represent an estimate of the best that could be done if the future climate were known in advance. The analysis focuses on a small number of PF strategies because of the computational intensity required by the optimization calculations,

Figure 6.1 Flow of Perfect Foresight and Robust Adaptation Analyses

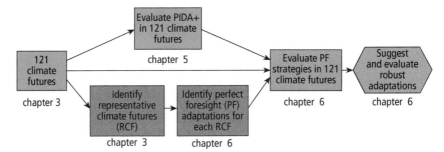

which are described in chapter 2. In this chapter, the analysis evaluates each PF strategy across the full range of 121 climate futures and uses this information to suggest potential robust adaptations for each basin using two robust criteria. The criteria aim to reduce the regret associated with infrastructure investments in an uncertain climate, that is, to reduce the difference in lost revenues between the investments made and what might have been chosen with perfect information about future climate. The chapter then reports on the performance of these robust adaptation strategies.

Perfect Foresight Adaptation

As described in chapter 2, the perfect foresight adaptations examine potential adjustments to the PIDA+ infrastructure in each basin to maximize the net present value (NPV) of hydropower production (revenues less cost of infrastructure changes), given constraints on allocating water to environmental flows, municipal use, industrial demands, and irrigation. At the basin level, the PF adaptations can adjust the planned turbine capacity, reservoir storage, and mean conveyance irrigation efficiency. As shown in table 2.2, the analysis assumes that turbine capacity can increase or decrease relative to PIDA+, efficiency can only increase, and reservoir storage can only decrease because engineering constraints limit the maximum size. At the farm level, the PF adaptations can adjust the planned irrigation area, employ deficit irrigation, and enhance mean field-level irrigation efficiency. When no other options are sufficient, the analysis also allows crop imports at the International Food Policy Research Institute's world market prices to maintain production levels. As shown in table 2.2, planned irrigation areas can increase or decrease, deficit and mean field-level efficiency can only increase, and imports can only increase relative to PIDA+.

The six representative climate futures were chosen to span the range of wetter and drier future climate conditions in each of the seven basins studied, so the PF adaptations show the range of potential responses to these conditions. The optimization procedure that generates each PF adaptation is described in more detail in chapter 2 and fully documented in online appendix B.[1] Because the six climate futures manifest differently in each basin, the optimal adaptation investment profile also differs by basin. In general, however, in wetter conditions the PF adaptations tend to expand turbine capacity to generate more hydropower from the additional water available. In drier conditions, the PF adaptations tend to reduce turbine capacity and increase irrigation efficiency in response to reduced water resources.

These PF adaptations can reduce the potential losses from climate change and take advantage of potential windfall gains, although their effectiveness varies among the basins. Figure 6.2 shows an estimate of the maximum percentage change in present value revenues from hydropower revenues for the PF adaptations in a changing climate relative to those available for PIDA+ with the historical climate in each basin. The 0 percent benchmark in the figure represents the revenues of PIDA+ with the historical climate. For each basin, the left part of the bar shows, as a percentage of no-climate-change revenues, the gains with adaptation in the driest scenario (stemming from reducing the losses that would

Figure 6.2 Gains from Perfect Foresight Adaptations: Hydropower
(US$, billions)

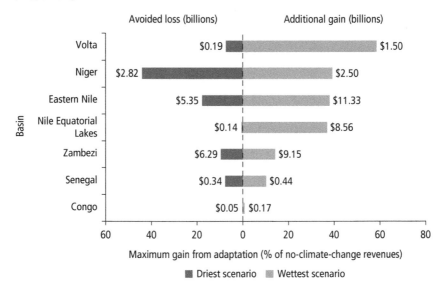

have prevailed if baseline investment plans were not modified). The right part of the bar in each basin represents the gains with adaptation in the wettest scenario. These would come from the additional hydropower generated by increasing the generation capacity to take advantage of the larger volume of water available.

Overall, these results suggest that in each basin, adaptation has great potential to alleviate the losses and expand the opportunities of climate change. For example, adaptation in the Zambezi basin has great potential to alleviate losses—gaining back US$6.3 billion of potential losses in a dry scenario and adding US$9.1 billion in gains in wetter scenarios—as does adaptation in the Senegal basin. The Nile and Volta basins have high "upside" adaptation potential, as infrastructure performance in wet scenarios can be markedly increased through adaptation, but much less potential for adaptation in dry scenarios. The potential for adaptation to reduce losses and increase gains is reviewed for all the basins in table 6.1, covering hydropower and irrigation expansions.

It is important to note that the PF adaptations considered here do not represent any recommended adaptation for the basins. An optimization tool such as that used in this study necessarily makes simplifying assumptions about specific facilities, either current or planned; the range of plausible adaptations at each facility; and the specific costs and prices that could define a truly optimal path.

Table 6.1 NPV of Investment in Hydropower and Irrigation Expansion, without and with Perfect Foresight Adaptation, 2015–50
(US$, billions)

Basin	PV without climate change	Max PV reduction due to CC (worst scenario)	Max PV gain due to CC (best scenario)	NPV for best adaptation for worst scenario	NPV for best adaptation for best scenario	Max adaptation gain for worst climate (reduction of losses)	Max adaptation gain for best climate (additional gains)
Congo	156.2	−16.62	0.93	139.63	157.3	0.05	0.17
Niger	195.31	−9.11	8.07	211.73	234.39	25.53	31.01
Eastern Nile	73.76	−13.45	18.25	65.36	104.38	5.05	12.37
Nile Equatorial	28.7	−13.32	11.48	18.08	48.11	2.7	7.93
Senegal	42.55	−3.82	0.88	46.73	51.92	8	8.49
Volta	28.21	−7.05	28.63	21.16	69.45	0	12.61
Zambezi	87.52	−45.01	15.66	53.73	116.62	11.22	13.44
All basins	612.25	−66.946	46.115	n.a.	n.a.	n.a.	n.a.

Note: The all basins totals in columns two and three are not a simple sum of the basin maximum reductions or maximum gains, because each basin's worst and best climate future can differ. The totals are less than the simple sum, because they reflect the worst and best basin climate futures applied consistently over all basins. CC = climate change; NPV = net present value; n.a. = not applicable.

In addition, the study team lacked specific information about the engineering, economic, and political constraints in each basin that affect the choice of water and energy infrastructure that might be available to local planners. Local planning bodies, such as water basin authorities, could adopt an approach similar to that used here but incorporating all the details necessary to recommend a particular investment plan. The results in this study aim to illustrate how a search for an alternative investment profile can suggest infrastructure investments that would be more resilient to future climate change, to demonstrate the potential of adaptation to reduce losses and exploit opportunities presented by climate change, and to quantify that potential to a first approximation.

Benefit of Perfect Foresight Adaptations across Climate Futures

Table 6.1 summarizes the maximum potential gains from adaptation. It is useful to consider how these gains vary in each basin across the full range of 121 climate futures. Figure 6.3 shows such an evaluation for two basins, the Volta and the Zambezi. This figure presents results for hydropower only, which, as illustrated in chapter 4, is by far the most important contributor to the total PV of water infrastructure in the Zambezi basin. The 121 climate futures are arrayed along the horizontal axis, with the wettest to the left and the driest to the right. The vertical axis is normalized (at 100) to the no-climate-change revenues. Red bars in the figure show the contribution of climate to revenues—so bars that extend above the 100 line represent potential windfalls and those below, potential losses. The role of the best PF adaptation (one of the six strategies examined) is represented by the green portion of the bars, which in some cases provides additional gains (the group to the left); in some cases, it provides a reversal of loss (the group in the center); and in some cases, it provides reduced damages. The profile of these three groups varies by basin, as indicated by the comparison of the results for Zambezi and Volta in the figure.

Figure 6.4 provides a similar analysis for the same two basins, but focuses on irrigation. Panel a, for Zambezi, shows a relative insensitivity of irrigation to climate and little variation in the role of adaptation. Volta shows much more variation across climates. One implication is that the regrets from choosing a particular adaptation strategy, when performance varies so markedly, can be higher in cases like Volta.

A different story on the value of adaptation emerges for the Volta basin in the West African Power Pool (WAPP). In most climate futures, the economic performance of infrastructure is greater under climate change than under the historical climate. In some futures, the net value of adaptation in the Volta basin is more than 50 percent of the baseline economic performance.

Figure 6.3 Estimates of the Economic Value of Investing in Climate Change Adaptation, for the Zambezi and Volta Basins: Hydropower Only

(No-climate-change revenues = 100)

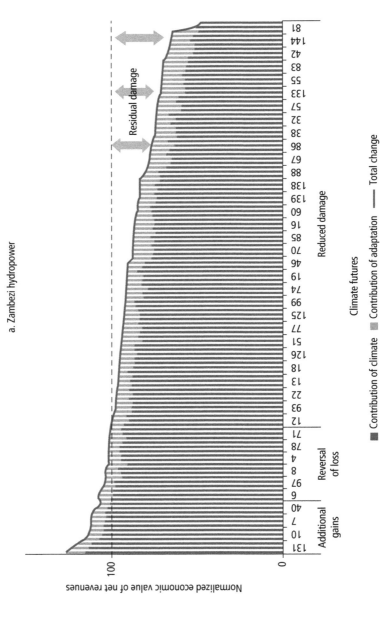

a. Zambezi hydropower

b. Volta hydropower

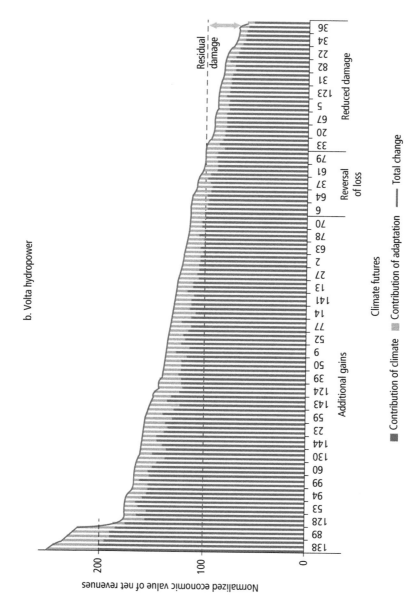

Climate futures

■ Contribution of climate ▨ Contribution of adaptation —— Total change

Note: The values in the graphs are normalized values. Numbers on the x-axis are the climate future codes.

Figure 6.4 Estimates of the Economic Value of Investing in Climate Change Adaptation for the Zambezi and Volta Basins: New PIDA+ Irrigation Facilities

(No-climate-change revenues = 100)

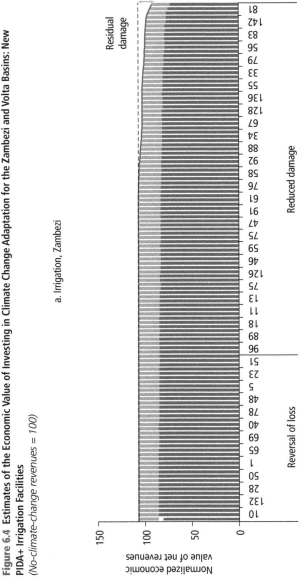

a. Irrigation, Zambezi

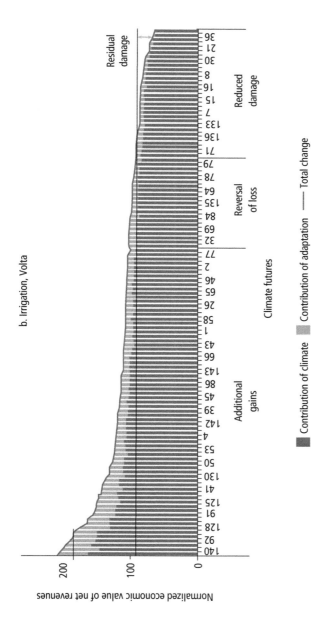

b. Irrigation, Volta

Normalized economic value of net revenues

Climate futures

Residual damage · Reduced damage · Reversal of loss · Additional gains

■ Contribution of climate   ■ Contribution of adaptation   —— Total change

Note: Values in the graphs are normalized values (no-climate-change revenues = 100). Numbers on the x-axis are the climate future codes. In the Zambezi basin, PIDA+ and the best PF adaptation have lower value in most climate futures than does PIDA+ in the historical climate. These gains are at least US$4 billion, and perhaps as much as US$10 billion, depending on the climate future. A US$10 billion gain from investing in adaptation corresponds to roughly one-third of the total present value of all new infrastructure revenues in the historical case.

Regretting Adaptation When the Future Climate Is Unknown

Up to now, the results we have presented reflect an important implicit assumption—that a basin-level planner has perfect foresight about which climate future will arise. That assumption is unrealistic, as in fact the basin-level planner faces uncertainty about which climate future will come to pass. With that uncertainty comes the risk that an adaptation strategy tuned to a particular climate turns out to be maladaptive to other climate outcomes. While ignoring climate change entails serious risks of planning and designing infrastructure that is not suited for the climate of the future, there is also a risk of adapting to climate change in the "wrong" way, which could be as significant, or more, than the risk of incurring damages when not adapting. A regrets-laden, wrong adaptation decision takes place, for example, when it is based on the expectation that the future will be drier, when, in fact, it turns out to be wetter. Each of the six optimal adaptation strategies identified in response to a particular climate future carries the risk of generating damages (or "regrets") when a different climate materializes. In the Zambezi basin, for example, basin planners can ignore climate change when planning hydropower and later regret that decision, as it can generate a loss of about 18 percent of baseline revenues; but if they adapt in the wrong way, they can face a regret of close to 30 percent of baseline revenues (figure 6.5).

Although the results in figures 6.2, 6.3, and 6.4 usefully demonstrate the potential value of adaptation, it is nonetheless important to look at the outcomes of each of these PF strategies as the planner would, with the ex ante perspective that the infrastructure they build in the near term could ultimately face any of a range of

Figure 6.5 Damage from Not Adapting or Misadapting Hydropower Expansion Plans

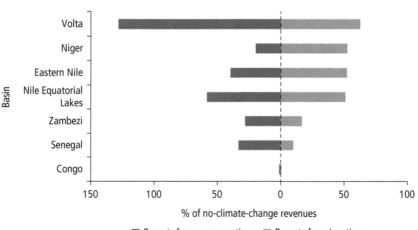

climate futures as represented by the 121 futures considered in this analysis. Accordingly, figure 6.6 compares the regret of each of the PF adaptations for the Zambezi and Volta basins across the full range of 121 climate futures.

As discussed in chapter 2, the regret of a strategy in any future is the difference between its performance and the best-performing strategy in that future.

Figure 6.6 Regret of PIDA+ and Perfect Foresight Adaptations across the Range of Climate Futures for the Zambezi and Volta Basins

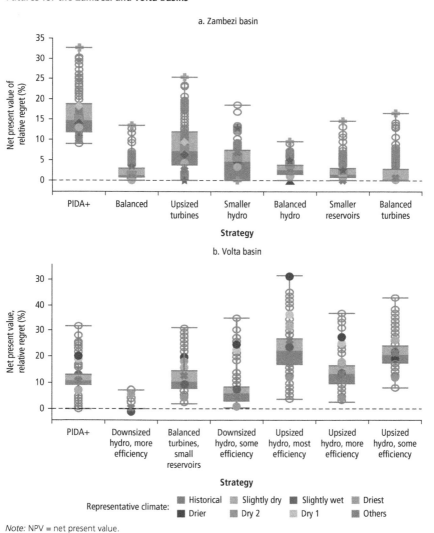

Note: NPV = net present value.

That is, the regret measures the difference in NPV between the strategy one chooses under uncertainty and the strategy one could have chosen with perfect information about the future. Ideally, one can identify a strategy with small regrets, one that performs well over a wide range of futures. The horizontal axis in figure 6.6 lists the seven investment strategies considered in each basin: PIDA+ and the investments generated by the perfect foresight calculations for the six representative climate futures. The vertical axis shows the *relative* regret for each strategy. The relative regret is a ratio, with the numerator being the regret for a particular climate outcome of the 121 (that is, the NPV "penalty" relative to the best possible outcome if the planner had perfect foresight) and the denominator being the NPV for the best possible outcome for that scenario. Considering relative regrets suggests the importance of a well-tailored adaptation in each basin relative to the overall scale of investment. Clearly, a US$5 billion regret is more consequential in a basin where the best possible NPV is US$10 billion than one where the best possible NPV is US$100 billion. Figure 6.6 uses box-and-whisker plots to show the range of relative regret for each investment. The colored dots show the regrets for the historical climate and the representative climate futures.

For the Zambezi basin, the box-and-whisker plot for the no-adaptation PIDA+ strategy indicates that 90 percent of the outcomes yield relative regrets from 5 percent to almost 16 percent, but 50 percent of the outcomes are clustered in the 7 to 10 percent range. The upsized turbines strategy yields the broadest range of regrets, with the extreme possibility of a 25 percent regret at the high end. But, like the other perfect foresight strategies, the upsized turbines strategy also has the potential to yield 0 percent regret (if Climate 80, the slightly wet climate future, is the one that manifests). The balanced hydro strategy, with a balance of strategically upsized and downsized hydropower capacities, has a much narrower range of regrets.

For the Volta basin, there is much more variation in relative regrets across all the strategies. At least one of the perfect foresight strategies, upsized hydro with most efficiency, a high adaptation investment scenario, is riskier than the others, and riskier than PIDA+. The source of the risk with this upsized hydro strategy is a large expansion in hydropower capacity, which could lead to substantial gains in hydropower production in very wet scenarios, but it could also lead to high infrastructure construction costs in other scenarios. The downsized hydro with more efficiency strategy, second from the left in figure 6.6, panel b, minimizes regrets for the largest number of scenarios. But the strategy implies a scaling back of hydropower capacities, which may carry other implications for basin-scale planners.

The results presented here provide important inputs to the decision-making process, quantifying the economic regrets of various alternative strategies. Nonetheless, the results for the Volta and Zambezi basins suggest that planners need to consider all the implications of adaptation, including economic, social, and political, in thinking through robust strategies for adapting to climate change. These results also make clear that planning without consideration of climate change should not be advised—the gains to adaptation need at least to be considered in the decision-making process.

Robust Adaptation

We can now use this information to compare the robustness of the alternative PF strategies and suggest which adaptations are most robust, that is, which adaptations might be attractive to planners who understand the climate is changing but do not have good information about what specific climate their basin will face in the future. Several different definitions of robustness are used in the decision making and planning literatures, but all emphasize the idea of strategies that perform well over a wide range of plausible futures or, at least, have limited downside risk if the future turns out differently than expected. In this study, we use two robustness criteria to capture these ideas. The most robust PF strategy in any basin is the strategy that: (a) minimizes the maximum regret or (b) minimizes the 75th percentile regret.

The first criterion is the traditional mini-max regret criterion (Savage 1954), which is easy to implement but can be unduly influenced by extreme cases. The second criterion is a variant of what is known in the literature as the domain criterion (Schneller and Sphicas 1983), in which the most robust strategy has regret less than some threshold value across the widest range of futures. In our implementation, we set the threshold value at the 75th percentile regret of the best-performing strategy. This domain criterion is less sensitive to the extreme cases than mini-max, and is particularly useful when no reliable probabilistic information exists about alternative futures.[1] Any difference between the two robustness criteria considered provides information on the extent to which a few extreme cases drive the results.

Table 6.2 shows the most robust of the PF strategies with the two criteria for each of the seven basins. For all but two basins (Nile and Zambezi), these criteria suggest the same robust strategy for each basin. The strategy that minimizes the 75th percentile regrets in the Zambezi, designed to adapt to a drier climate with balanced hydropower capacity changes, has the smallest range in figure 6.6. In all but the Nile basin, the most robust strategy is designed for a somewhat drier climate than the historical climate. This finding suggests that the regret for the basin operator resulting from overinvesting, that is, planning for a wetter than realized climate, is higher than the regret resulting from lost opportunities, that is, planning for a drier than realized climate. In the Nile Equatorial Lakes region, the most robust strategy over the widest range of climates (Drier – 90)

Table 6.2 Robust Strategies for Each Basin and Their Performance Compared with PIDA+

Basin	Robust strategy		Regret of robust strategy		NPV of PIDA+ revenues, historical climate (US$, billions)	PIDA+ regrets		Robust strategy compared with PIDA+	
	Maximum regret	75% highest regret	Max regret (US$, billions)	75% highest regret (US$, billions)		Max regret (US$, billions)	Min regret (US$, billions)	Max regret reduced (%)	Range of high regret climates reduced (%)
Congo	Dry (124)	Dry (124)	0.7	0.7	156	0.9	0.0	14	14
Niger	Drier (80)	Drier (80)	0.0	0.0	195	31.9	25.5	100	100
Eastern Nile	Wettest (137)	Wettest (137)	3.8	3.8	74	17.0	5.1	78	—
Nile Equatorial Lakes	Wetter (39)	Drier (90)	4.5	7.6	29	12.9	0.7	65	—
Senegal	Dry (124)	Dry (124)	0.6	0.6	43	8.5	7.9	93	2
Volta	Driest (35)	Driest (35)	2.1	2.1	28	16.1	0.0	87	87
Zambezi	Dry 2 (124)	Drier (90)	7.1	7.7	88	16.1	8.1	56	12

Note: Numbers in parentheses are the scenario numbers. — = not available.

follows this pattern, but actually involves upsizing turbine capacity in response, reinforcing the need to take a careful look at basin-specific characteristics in assessing robust options, including temporal and spatial dimensions of climate futures that are difficult to summarize in a single metric (such as the seasonal pattern of rainfall). Interestingly, the most robust option with the mini-max criterion for the Nile Equatorial Lakes basin is a response to a wetter than historical climate, but the actual strategy underlying that option is also to upsize turbine capacity, albeit in a different spatial pattern across the new hydropower capacity.

In some basins, the robust strategy has small regret, which means that a single investment strategy performs well across all the climate projections considered. In other basins, the maximum regret of the robust PF strategy remains significant, which means that none of the strategies considered performs well across all the climates. In addition, the difference between the mini-max strategy and the satisficing strategy is generally small, which indicates that the extremely wet or dry cases do not play an important factor in our analysis.

To consider the benefits of these robust PF strategies, we can compare them with the PIDA+. As discussed above, a direct comparison of the NPVs of the PIDA+ and PF strategies is not appropriate. The PIDA+ investments aim to serve many purposes, such as flood control and peak power generation, which are not included in the economic measures considered in this study. To fully assess PIDA+ would require conducting a multi-attribute analysis beyond that conducted here. But we can usefully compare the extent to which the most robust PF strategy in each basin reduces the sensitivity of the PIDA+ investments to climate change. As shown in the previous charts, the calculated NPVs of each basin's PIDA+ investments vary, sometimes significantly, across the range of climate projections. We can use two measures to evaluate the ability of the alternative PF adaptation strategies to reduce this sensitivity: (a) the reduction in maximum regret relative to the PIDA+ strategy and (b) the reduction in the number of high-regret cases relative to PIDA+. In general, these two measures correlate reasonably well and thus suggest similar rankings among the basins of benefits from the robust PF strategies.

To support these measures, table 6.2 shows the maximum and minimum regrets for the PIDA+ strategy in each basin, along with the NPV for the PIDA+ strategy with the historical climate. For the first measure, the table shows the percentage reduction in maximum regret, as a fraction of the PIDA+ NPV, from the robust strategy compared with the PIDA+ strategy. For instance, in the Volta basin, the new PIDA+ investments have an NPV of US$28 billion with the historical climate. The maximum regret for these new PIDA+ investments is US$16 billion, while the maximum regret of the most robust PF investment in the Volta is US$2.1 billion. The robust investment thus reduces the maximum regret by 87 percent of the PIDA+ NPV. In contrast, the NPV of new PIDA+ investments in the Congo basin is US$156 billion and the maximum regret of the PIDA+ is just less than US$1 billion. The robust investments do not significantly reduce this regret.

Figure 6.7 compares the relative regret for the PIDA+ and robust adaptation investments. The chart excludes the Orange basin, whose PIDA+ plans do not include any significant new infrastructure investments, as discussed in chapter 4. The total bar for each basin shows the maximum relative regret for PIDA+ over the 121 climate futures; the lower (orange) part of the bar shows the maximum relative regret for the robust adaptation. The difference between the two, indicated by the blue region, is the maximum reduction in regret obtained by the robust adaption in each basin. The orange region is the residual regret that cannot be eliminated by any of the PF strategies considered in this study.

Figure 6.8 adopts the same approach, but considers the impact of the robust option in reducing irrigation regrets. The robust strategy is more effective at reducing irrigation regrets than hydropower regrets, which is in part a function of the objective function that was applied in searching for the robust strategy. That is, the objective function seeks to find options that maximize hydropower, subject to the constraint of holding agricultural production as close to current levels as possible. In addition, there is a greater adaptation opportunity set for irrigation, so there are more possibilities to reduce regret with a robust adaptation alternative.

Figure 6.7 Benefits of Robust Adaptation Compared with PIDA+ in Each Basin: Hydropower Only

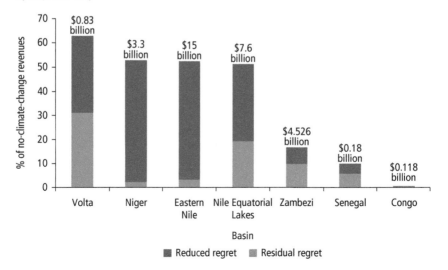

Figure 6.8 Benefits of Robust Adaptation Compared with PIDA+ in Each Basin: Irrigation Only

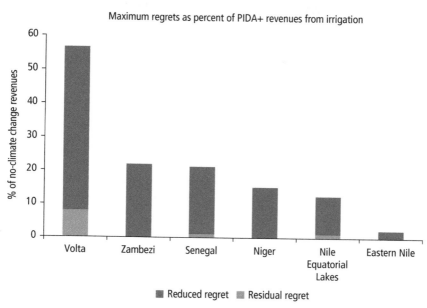

Maximum regrets as percent of PIDA+ revenues from irrigation

■ Reduced regret ■ Residual regret

For the second measure, table 6.2 also shows the range of regrets for the PIDA+ investments and for the most robust PF strategy. The range of regrets for the former is given by the difference between the maximum and minimum regret for each strategy. For instance, the Volta PIDA+ investments have a US$16.1 billion range of regrets across the set of climate projections, as seen by the difference between the maximum and minimum regret column values. The range of regrets for the PF strategies is the same as the maximum regret, since the minimum regret is zero. The ratio of the range of regrets between the robust PF and PIDA+ strategies thus provides another measure of how much the former reduces any sensitivity to climate change. The right-most column of table 6.2 provides these values. In some basins, such as the Volta, the robust PF strategy eliminates much of the sensitivity to climate change, while in other basins, such as the Zambezi, the PIDA+ strategy has significant sensitivity to climate change, but the robust PF strategy eliminates only a portion of that variation.

Inside Robust Adaptation

The previous analysis suggests significant benefits from modifying the PIDA+ investment plans to make them more robust across a wide range of climate futures. In practice, what would it entail to adopt a robust adaptation strategy? Figure 6.9 provides a visual summary of the changes in the variables chosen in this analysis to represent key decisions to be made by basin planners when expanding water and power infrastructure.

The chart is divided into three regions, one on the left showing changes in conveyance efficiency for each basin, one on the right showing changes in turbine capacity, and one in the middle showing changes in reservoir storage. The vertical axis indicates the percentage of the corresponding investment increases, decreases, or no changes between the robust adaptation and PIDA+ for each basin. The legend indicates "large decreases" (the largest changes for each category of lever in table 2.2, for example, a 50 percent reduction in turbine capacity) and "large increases" (the largest increases from table 2.2, for example, a 50 percent increase in turbine capacity).

The changes are weighted, for each variable, by the corresponding baseline value: area for conveyance, volume for storage, and megawatts for

Figure 6.9 Changes in Baseline Investments under Robust Adaptation

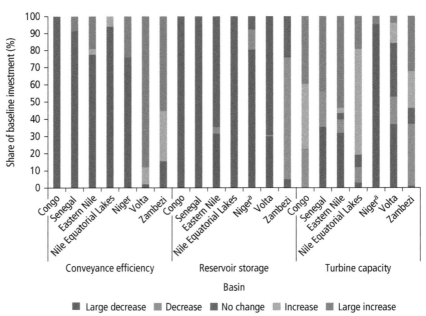

Note: For conveyance efficiency, a large increase is up to 95 percent, an increase is up to 85 percent, both from a 75 percent baseline; for reservoir storage, a large decrease is −50 percent, a decrease is −25 percent; for turbine capacity, a large increase/decrease is +/− 50 percent, and an increase/decrease is +/− 25 percent.
a. See box 6.1 for the explanation of Niger basin hydropower results.

turbine capacity. The analysis only considers potential increases in conveyance and potential decreases in storage, but both increases and decreases in turbine capacity.

The main message is that adaptation entails, overall, a significant departure from the decisions that would be made in the absence of climate change; however, there is considerable variation in the signs and magnitudes of change across basins and decision variables.

In some basins, such as the Congo basin, the robust adaption is largely similar to PIDA+, with no change in storage, increases in efficiency in only a small portion of the irrigated area, and changes to only a small fraction of the turbine capacity. These small differences are largely the result of excluding the Inga investments from the adaptation analysis, and also the fact that there is abundant water in the Congo; with climate change, water will almost certainly remain abundant. In other basins, such as the Zambezi, the robust adaptation is significantly different from PIDA+, with increases in efficiency over most of the irrigated area, decreases in storage capacity for a significant fraction of the projects, and changes (mostly increases) to almost the entire portfolio of new turbine capacity.

Cost of Adaptation

The increases in NPV for the robust adaptations considered in this study are calculated at the basin level. The NPV calculations are inclusive of any extra costs implied by these adaptations. However, the PIDA+ plans in each basin include investments by many different parties. Cost savings for some projects in a basin cannot in general be used to offset cost increases in other parts of the basin—these amounts are not fungible across projects. Thus, it is also useful to total the investment costs of projects in two categories, where costs increase or decrease for each robust adaptation relative to PIDA+. Figure 6.10 shows such changes for six basins. In general, in hydropower, cost increases and cost savings appear to be of similar orders of magnitude, mostly on the order of 10 to 20 percent of baseline investment costs, with some dominance of the cost increases. The exception is from the Niger basin, where the result is sensitive to assumptions on the relevant power pricing regime (see box 6.1 for a more detailed discussion).

Robust adaptation appears to be fully justified, even when only cost increases are considered. Comparing the latter with the benefit expressed as a reduction of the maximum regrets, the benefit/ cost ratio comfortably exceeds one in all basins—see the last column of table 6.3. The exception is from the Congo basin, confirming that in that basin the regrets from inaction may be too small to warrant significant departures from baseline investment plans.

Figure 6.10 Cost of Robust Adaptation for Hydropower

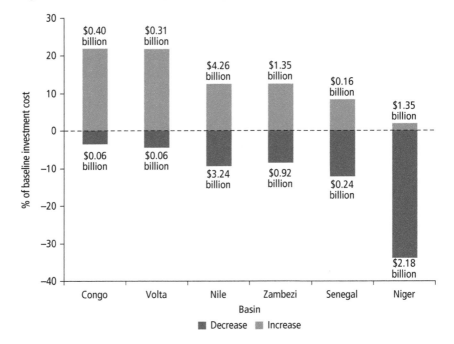

Benefits of Robust Adaptation to Electricity Consumers

Robust adaptation also has the potential to reduce consumer costs of electricity. Overall, compared with the no-adaptation case, electricity expenditure in dry scenarios decreases in virtually all countries. However, the effects are more noticeable in the Southern African Power Pool (SAPP) than in Eastern Africa Power Pool (EAPP) and especially the WAPP (figure 6.11).

Table 6.4 provides additional detailed insights for selected countries in each power pool. The table presents estimated absolute values of cumulative electricity costs to consumers by power pool and country. As noted earlier, costs without adaptation for the driest and wettest scenarios vary widely at the country level. But in each of the variants for the robust adaptation scenario, the costs of power are reduced relative to the no-adaptation driest scenario, in all cases but Nigeria, for which the costs are only slightly more. The reduction in costs is further evidence of the value of robust strategies in the face of climate change. In addition, the countries with the lowest vulnerability to climate change in the table (the Arab Republic of Egypt and Nigeria) have the ability to turn internally

BOX 6.1

Sensitivity Analysis for a Hydropower Peaking Plant: Niger Basin

In the general methodology of the analysis, as outlined in box 2.3 in chapter 2, there is no allowance for consideration of higher energy prices that might be envisioned for a facility designed for peaking load operation, or for other physical characteristics (such as turbine capacity or reservoir volume) of proposed hydropower that would be more suitable for a peaking load plant. This is because the study team did not have access, in general, to the detailed, facility-level information needed to determine if a particular plant is intended to produce peak or base load power. This level of detail was addressed as part of the Track 2 analysis (see chapter 7). As long as the peaking plants in the Track 1 analysis have relatively small capacities, the overall degree of error introduced by this simplification will generally be small.

There is one specific case in the Niger basin, the proposed 3,000 megawatts Mambila facility in southeastern Nigeria (representing roughly 65 percent of the proposed new hydropower production in the basin), in which the operation for base or peak load would make a difference for the basin as a whole.

As a result, the project team conducted a sensitivity analysis on the perfect foresight results for the Niger basin, using a higher price assumption and an adjustment to certain plant characteristics in the Water Evaluation and Planning (WEAP) system to emulate the operation of a peaking facility.

The sensitivity analysis indicated that the perfect foresight and robust adaptation results for the Niger basin are particularly sensitive to the standard Track 1 assumptions. This finding affects in particular the results presented in figure 6.9. The results for Niger in that figure indicate that the optimized adaptation for the robust strategy incorporates large decreases in reservoir storage and turbine capacity across the basin, reflecting a finding that the Mambila facility's turbine capacity and reservoir capacity are downsized by 50 percent under all six climate scenarios tested.

With altered electricity prices and the WEAP operational assumptions, however, the sensitivity analysis for turbine capacity shows that the Mambila capacity would be increased by 50 percent in the two wettest climate futures, decreased by 25 percent in two of the drier climate futures, and would remain at the proposed capacity in PIDA+ for the two other, more central climate futures. The pattern of responsiveness to climate in the sensitivity analysis is more typical of the infrastructure adjustments made for other facilities in the perfect foresight analysis. Although it was not possible in this study to incorporate a revised treatment of peaking facilities in the Niger basin or other basin modeling runs, in future work of this type these results suggest that particular care is needed when considering climate adaptive infrastructure design options for peaking load facilities.

Table 6.3 Costs and Benefits of Robust Adaptation

Basin	Increased cost (US$, billions)	Decreased cost (US$, billions)	Reduced maximum regret (US$, billions)	Benefit/cost ratio
Congo	0.40	0.06	0.12	0.29
Niger	1.35	2.18	3.30	2.45
Nile	4.26	3.24	22.60	5.31
Senegal	0.16	0.24	0.18	1.14
Volta	0.31	0.06	0.83	2.64
Zambezi	1.35	0.92	4.53	3.36

to fossil backstop technologies if hydropower performs below expectations, but other countries do not possess this flexibility.

Interestingly, at the power pool level, there are key countries that have potential alternatives to hydro that allow adaptation at lower costs. In the SAPP, South Africa has the potential to switch to coal to adapt to lower levels of hydro imports from Grand Inga. In WAPP and the EAPP, Egypt and Nigeria have potential gas alternatives. In other instances, such as in the EAPP, interconnections play an important role, allowing other low-cost, abundant renewables, such as geothermal power, to make up the shortfall in supply and trade in the region.

Role of Power Trade in Adaptation

On the continental scale, trade between countries within each power pool and between countries from different pools will play a critical role in adaptation to climate change. The potential for future hydropower generation is not evenly split across the river basins and power pools from a geographical point of view. Approximately 55 percent of new hydropower expansion is concentrated in the Congo River basin, in particular the Grand Inga project.

Further, several major demand centers are some distance from potential hydro investments. Egypt, Nigeria, and South Africa need to import either from neighbors or nearby regions to take advantage of low-cost hydro. According to the analysis, connecting these demand centers with hydro production centers in regional river basins has the potential to provide lower-cost electricity, with obvious benefits to end-consumers.

This study considers only committed and planned trade links between countries. The intent is to ensure a relatively conservative approach when modeling each country and power pool's energy system. In the case of the SAPP, where the effects of climate change are most noticeable, the model considers planned

Figure 6.11 **Effects of Robust Adaptation on Consumer Energy Expenditures**
(No-climate change = 100)

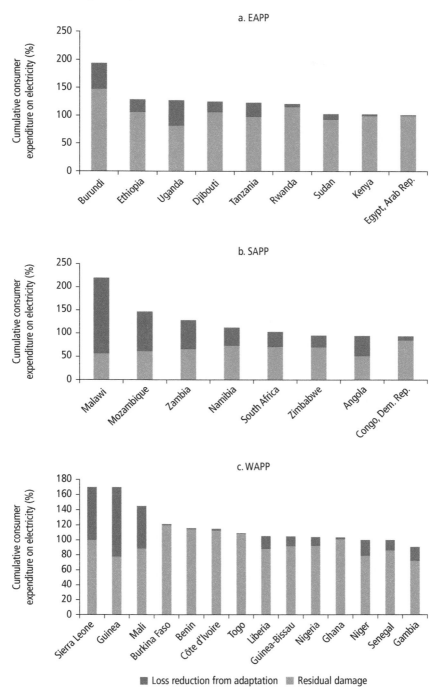

a. EAPP

b. SAPP

c. WAPP

■ Loss reduction from adaptation   ■ Residual damage

Table 6.4 Present Value of Consumer Expenditure on Electricity, without and with Robust Adaptation, 2015–50
(US$, billions)

Power pool and country	No climate change	No adaptation		Robust adaptation, designed to minimize:	
		Driest scenario	Wettest scenario	Maximum regret	75% highest regret
Southern African Power Pool					
South Africa	1,214.47	1,769.49	1,232.86	1,220.38	—
Malawi	6.27	19.54	5.72	5.01	4.96
West African Power Pool					
Mali	18.41	22.16	17.72	18.67	18.67
Nigeria	683.73	691.49	677.40	690.04	690.04
Eastern Africa Power Pool					
Tanzania	66.46	81.78	63.16	64.87	67.80
Egypt, Arab Rep.	1,716.04	1,732.03	1,711.62	1,715.19	1,714.87

Note: — = not available.

Figure 6.12 Total Electricity Exports vs. Hydropower Generation, SAPP

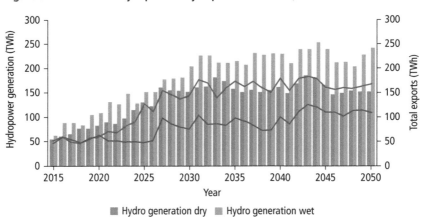

Hydro generation dry   Hydro generation wet

Note: SAPP = Southern African Power Pool; TWh = terawatt hours.

and committed trade links between the 12 Southern African countries, which amounts to a capacity of 20 gigawatts. Figures 6.12 and 6.13 provide insights as to the importance of developing intercountry transmission lines for electricity trade for this region. Representative "dry" and "wet" scenarios are considered. Even under the dry scenario, large volumes of electricity are traded, as shown in figure 6.12.

Figure 6.13 Cost of Electricity Comparison: Base, Dry, and Wet Scenarios

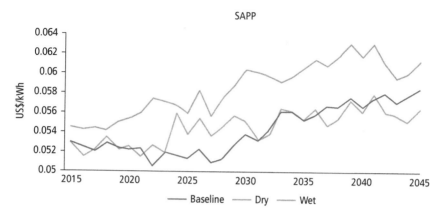

Note: kWh = kilowatt hours; SAPP = Southern African Power Pool.

The drop in hydro production in the dry scenario results in increased generation by coal fired and other power plants. In figure 6.13, the extra fuel cost is translated into higher regional production prices for electricity.

In summary, having (conservative) trade links in place can result in significant gains in wet climates. A difference in trade between 50 and 100 terawatt hours annually—the difference between the two extremes—in the latter part of the period results in approximately a 15 percent reduction in price. Yet even a dry scenario has well over 100 terawatt hours of hydropower trade. If the trade options were somehow removed (or stifled due to limited transmission investments), higher-cost impacts would be incurred.

Combination of Robust Decision Making and Adaptive Management

Adaptive management can be an additional component of a climate change response strategy. Although this topic is beyond the scope of the present report, it is worth describing what the features of such an approach would look like. Under adaptive management, the analysis would consider the potential benefits of learning as climate change unfolds. This would probably result in the identification of additional measures to reduce regrets, supplementing in each basin the six alternative investment strategies discussed earlier. In general, information generated in robust decision-making analyses can be used to help inform the design of such enhancements.

Figure 6.14 suggests how the analysis might proceed. The figure shows the change in the total amount of turbine capacity and reservoir storage in the Volta basin compared with PIDA+ for each of the six investment strategies. The figure also shows the increase in irrigation efficiency compared with PIDA+ for each strategy, for delivery and in the field. For instance, the strategy designed to respond to the driest climate, which involves downsized hydro (on the left in the figure), is the most robust strategy, but has 18 percent less turbine capacity and 15 percent less storage than PIDA+.

The strategy also increases delivery and field irrigation efficiencies by 6 and 39 percent, respectively. These changes seem consistent with a drier climate. As the climates grow wetter, moving from left to right in the figure, the main

Figure 6.14 Perfect Foresight Adaptation Strategies in Volta Basin Compared with PIDA+

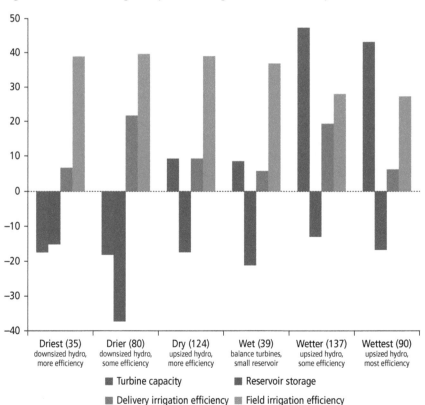

Note: All adaptation strategies shown are normalized to baseline levels or capacities.

change in the corresponding investment strategies tends to be an increase in turbine capacity. For instance, the strategy for the wettest climate, with upsized hydro (on the right in the figure), increases turbine capacity by 43 percent compared with PIDA+. This strategy also has similar storage as the downsized hydro strategy, and slightly less investment in delivery irrigation efficiency.

This pattern in PF strategies (moving from drier to wetter climates) suggests that an even more robust response to climate change in the Volta basin might include an adaptive management strategy, designed to evolve over time in response to new information. Such a strategy might begin with the reduced turbine capacity warranted under the driest scenario, but include the option of adding turbine capacity if subsequent information suggests the climate will be wetter. Planners might create such an option by designing the powerhouses and tunnels larger than needed for the initial turbines, to reduce the cost of subsequently adding additional turbines. An evaluation of such a strategy would need to balance the cost of these larger powerhouses and tunnels with the subsequent potential benefit of generating more hydropower in wetter climate futures. In addition, planners would have to consider whether they will be able to receive reliable scientific information in the future about the likelihood of drier or wetter climates in the Volta.

Another dimension of adaptive management might include enhancing power trade. The PIDA+ reference scenario assumptions for the Grand Inga system assume a staggered, and perhaps slower than technically feasible, new build program—with only 6 gigawatts of proposed transmission lines between the Democratic Republic of Congo and its neighboring countries in the SAPP. From a techno-economic perspective, an increase in trade capacity from and build out of Grand Inga in the Democratic Republic of Congo could benefit the countries not only in the SAPP, but also in the Central Africa Power Pool, EAPP, and WAPP. But realization of these benefits would require significant new transmission capacity investments, beyond those already signed and committed.

As indicated in figures 3.6, 3.7, and 3.8 in chapter 3, the Congo River basin is relatively unaffected by climate change in scenarios in which neighboring basins—such as the Volta and Niger—are more vulnerable. In the power pools of those basins, when hydropower is not available, natural gas is typically the next cheapest option and is used to generate electricity to meet shortfalls in dryer climates. However, allowing increased utilization of Grand Inga, and associated trade, would require lower levels of gas to be used for domestic generation. It would free up the natural gas resources to be used in higher-value activities on the one hand, while also lowering the production cost of electricity on the other.

Further, increased connectivity across power pools and between basins might yield important seasonal gains. For example, in the cases of two specific climate futures outlined in chapter 3 (numbers 90 and 39), countries around the

Equatorial Lakes sub-basin of the Nile experience sufficient rainfall. However, at the same time, countries around the Eastern Nile sub-basin experience low runoff. There is a case in this basin to increase transmission and export greater volumes of electricity from water-rich to simultaneously water-stricken regions. It may be the case that, at a larger regional scale, investments in selected transmission systems may help provide a powerful measure to climate-proof the continent's electricity sector. Although this study was not able to evaluate these options further, subsequent analyses in the region might extend and employ the modeling suite developed here to assess the robustness of trade-enhancing, interbasin transmission investments in a quantitative way.

Note

1. We also considered a 90 percent regret threshold, but the most robust strategy was generally the same as when applying the mini-max criterion.

References

Savage, L. J. 1954. *The Foundations of Statistics*. Mineola, NY: Dover Publications.

Schneller, G. O., and G. P. Sphicas. 1983. "Decision Making under Certainty: Starr's Domain Criterion." *Theory and Decision* 15: 321–36.

Chapter 7

Adaptation to Climate Change in Project Design

David Groves, Zhimin Mao, Rikard Liden, Kenneth M. Strzepek, Robert Lempert, Casey Brown, Mehmet Ümit Taner, and Evan Bloom

Project-Scale Analysis Overview: Scope of Adaptation

Whereas planning of infrastructure at the river basin and national scales is important for broad, long-term investment plans, the individual schemes are ultimately designed based on financial and economic analyses of the project-specific costs and benefits. The need for planning long-lived infrastructure projects by taking into account climate change has been highlighted often in recent times. Much emphasis has been placed on understanding the ensemble of future possible climate scenarios and how these would affect the performance of hydropower or irrigation projects. However, when attempting to utilize the complex information on climate futures to adapt the detailed design of such infrastructure, there has been a "culture clash" between climate scientists and engineers. One reason is that, in its level of detail, the design of a large water infrastructure project is equally, or even more, complex than the climate scenarios, considering the variety of technical aspects involved (e.g., geotechnical, hydraulic, mechanical, environmental, and social). Because of its unique dependence on site-specific characteristics and typically high demand for reliability in water delivery (e.g., power and water supply), large infrastructure project design is seldom based solely on financial or economic considerations, but on a combination of conservative safety margins, practical constraints for construction, and economic performance. The introduction of climate change uncertainty into this project design paradigm creates challenges, which are often underestimated by climate scientists and design engineers. The work presented in this chapter is an attempt to address the challenges of incorporating climate science into project design.

The suggested approach developed and tested in this report is an alternative to delivering one final design based on historical climate and hydrological records early in the process. Instead, the approach evaluates the effects of a broad spectrum of possible future climate projections on key performance metrics, for different basic design options. This will give the experienced dam engineer an indication of which direction for a specific design parameter (e.g., size of reservoir) is more robust to future potential climate change. Because such illustration is conducted early in the preparation process, its purpose is mainly to guide the process, rather than provide the final design. Although, for practical engineering reasons, one or only a few hydrology series must be chosen for conducting the whole chain of assessments in a feasibility study, the illustration of robustness to alternative climate futures could be an important input for the final decision on the design and the financial solutions for the project.

The main aim of this report is the development of a methodology and its testing in different geographic settings. It was not possible to make this experiment a part of ongoing feasibility studies. The report therefore presents independent, rapid analyses that were conducted based on limited data from existing completed prefeasibility and feasibility reports. It is therefore important to note that the detailed results regarding optimal design for the five test projects presented in this chapter are of less validity than the designs proposed by the feasibility study consultants, because the latter have access to a broader set of site-specific information.[1] However, the authorities and developers of the five test projects can get an indication from this report about the climate vulnerability of the proposed projects and whether further detailed integration of climate scenarios may be needed in the final design of the projects.

Choice of Methodology and Test Projects

To enable the assessment of the robust decision-making (RDM) method at the project scale, case studies were chosen from existing projects under preparation in Africa. The analyses take data from completed prefeasibility or feasibility analyses and examine alternative project designs using simple, stylized water planning models and cost models. Similar to the common approach in preparatory studies, the five projects are each "ring fenced" by isolating them from the overall basin context in which they are situated. Each test project thus treats upstream conditions and operations as fixed and as boundary conditions for the analysis. Because of this, and other simplifications, the findings are not intended as definitive statements regarding the benefits of alternative project designs. Rather, this study's analyses serve the following purposes:

- First, the case studies provide a basis for concluding under what conditions other projects could find value, or not, from including a full climate change robustness analysis in the feasibility study.

- Second, the analysis of the case studies offers analytical methods and tools that others can use to conduct similar screening studies for other projects.
- Third, the comparison among the five cases offers some allessons regarding the potential impacts of climate change on specific water infrastructure projects in Africa and initial indications as to the types of projects that might be most affected.

This report considers five test projects distributed across Sub-Saharan Africa, as shown in map 7.1. These test projects were chosen to span most of the broader African study area and reflect a variety of different project types—such as dams with storage, run-of-the-river dams, and transfer tunnels—and objectives—such as hydropower, irrigation, and urban water supply (box 7.1).

These projects are as follows:

1. *Lower Fufu Hydropower Project (Zambezi River Basin, Malawi).* This is a proposed run-of-the-river hydropower facility to be built within the Rukuru River watershed in northern Malawi.

Map 7.1 Test Project Locations

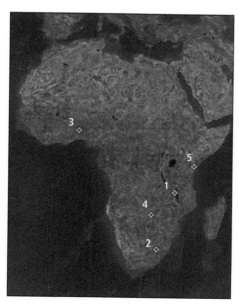

1. Lower Fufu Hydropower Project (Zambezi River basin, Malawi)

2. Polihali Dam and Conveyance Project (Orange River basin, Lesotho)

3. Pwalugu Multi-Purpose Dam Project (Volta River basin, Ghana)

4. Batoka Gorge Hydropower Project (Zambezi River basin, Zambia/Zimbabwe)

5. Mwache Dam and Reservoir Project (Kwale district, Kenya)

BOX 7.1

Test Project Descriptions

Lower Fufu (Malawi)
The Lower Fufu Hydropower Project is a proposed run-of-the-river hydropower facility to be built within the Rukuru River watershed in northern Malawi. A prefeasibility report was released in 1996 by Norconsult (Norconsult 1996). The basic scheme diverts water from two rivers—the North Rumphi and the South Rukuru—via two small concrete intake dams and two tunnels to a single hydropower turbine complex. The combined discharge flow is released into Lake Malawi.

The prefeasibility design calls for two tunnels of equal size to convey up to 31 cubic meters per second (m³/s) of total flow to the power generation facility. The design hydropower capacity is 90 megawatts (MW), and its capital cost in current dollars is estimated to be US$290 million. The power generated is expected to supply the Malawi power grid through a 132 kilovolt (kv) transmission line to the Bwengu region of Malawi. Subsequent documents by the World Bank suggest that the design could possibly be increased to accommodate a 200 MW hydropower facility.

Polihali
The Polihali dam is part of the second phase of the Lesotho Highlands Water Project (LHWP). It is described in a feasibility study commissioned by the Lesotho Highlands Water Commission (Consult 4 Consortium and SEED Consult 2007). The Polihali dam would be located downstream of the Khubelu and Senqu Rivers. The main objective of the project is to transfer water from Polihali reservoir to the existing Katse reservoir.

The LHWP has been found to be the least-cost alternative for supplying the growing water demand of the Gauteng area in South Africa. South Africa and Lesotho have thus agreed on the development and shared benefit of the LHWP. The first phase (the Katse and Mohale Dams, and water transfers) has already been completed, and the second phase (Polihali) is under preparation.

The Polihali Dam and reservoir proposed in the feasibility report has gross reservoir storage of 2,322 million cubic meters (MCM). A 38.2 kilometer (km) long tunnel from Polihali to Katse reservoir is sized to convey a maximum flow of about 35 m³/s to ensure an average yield of 14.75 m³/s over a year, or 465 MCM/year. The tunnel would be operated at full capacity for only a portion of the year. The average annual inflow to the site is 697 million m³/year.

Pwalugu
In 1992, the Volta River Authority commissioned a prefeasibility report to assess the economic and technical viability of three potential sites along the Volta River in Ghana for multipurpose dam projects—Pwalugu, Kulpaen, and Daboya (Volta River Authority 1993). The study recommended the Pwalugu site, located 30 kilometers southwest of Bolgatanga, as the most viable first investment of the three. The main benefits of the

(continued next page)

Box 7.1 (continued)

dam and reservoir project would be electricity production, irrigation water supply for new agricultural lands, and development of a lake fishery industry.

The prefeasibility report calls for a dam 41 meters high, to limit the flooded area and extent of community displacement and forest inundation. The reservoir would have gross storage of 4,200 MCM. Electricity would be produced using two generating units with a combined capacity of 48 MW. The power station would have a maximum turbine flow of 170 m^3/s, with average hydropower generation of 184 gigawatt hours (GWh)/year. The prefeasibility report estimates that the water yield for irrigation from the reservoir would be 2,200 million m^3/year. Using estimates of the average irrigation water requirement of 20,000 m^3/year for each hectare (ha), the project would support 110,000 ha of irrigated land, including more than 20,000 ha of rice farmland and 68,000 ha of improved pastoral land. The irrigation land area would be ramped up over a 15-year period and would use a gravity conveyance system with booster pumping stations.

Batoka Gorge

In 1992, the Zambezi River Authority (1993) commissioned a feasibility study to assess the economic and technical viability of hydropower development at 18 locations on the Zambezi River. The study recommended the Batoka Hydroelectric Scheme to be located 50 kilometers downstream of Victoria Falls. The main benefit of the hydropower project would be electricity production to supply markets in Zambia and Zimbabwe, within the Southern African Power Pool.

The feasibility report calls for a 181-meter-high roller-compacted concrete gravity arch dam, which would create a reservoir with gross storage of 1,680 million m^3. Two underground powerhouses (north and south) would contain four turbines each of 200 MW, fed by two penstocks. The power station would have a total installed capacity of 1,600 MW, a rated flow of 138.8 m^3/s, and produce on average 8,739 GWh/year, under historical hydrological conditions. Due to the limitations of this test project, which cannot analyze the full cascade and power system, the Batoka Gorge is evaluated as being mainly a base load power generation plant, ignoring other additional benefits.

Mwache

Urban water needs in Mombasa, Kenya, are projected to grow rapidly in the coming decades. The 2013 Water Supply Master Plan for Mombasa (Tahal Group 2013) identifies a range of water supply projects to meet these demand increases, including a dam on the Mwache River. The Mwache Dam is designed to provide 186,000 m^3/day of supply, with excess supply to be used for irrigation in nearby areas (for a total of 220,000 m^3/day).

The reservoir was initially designed at a height of 85 meters above ground level, for gross capacity of 200 MCM and a dead storage volume of 4 MCM. After discussions with World Bank experts, the dam height, gross capacity, and dead storage volume were adjusted to 65 meters, 120 MCM, and 20 MCM, respectively (Tahal Group 2013).

2. *Polihali Dam and Conveyance Project (Orange River basin, Lesotho).* Part of the second phase of the Lesotho Highlands Water Project, the Polihali dam would be located downstream of the Khubelu and Senqu Rivers, with the main objective of the project being to transfer water from a new reservoir to the existing Katse reservoir.

3. *Pwalugu Multipurpose Dam Project (Volta River basin, Ghana).* This is a dam and reservoir project designed to provide electricity production, irrigation water supply for new agricultural lands, flood control, and the development of a lake fishery industry.

4. *Batoka Gorge Hydropower Project (Zambezi River basin, Zambia/Zimbabwe).* This is a large, complex project that will support power generation in Zambia and Zimbabwe, and likely be linked to the transmission network of the Southern African Power Pool.

5. *Mwache Dam and Reservoir Project (Kwale district, Kenya).* This is a reservoir project designed to provide municipal water supply, with excess supply to be used for irrigation in nearby areas.

The projects are located in regions with significantly different hydrological conditions (figure 7.1). Three of the project areas (Lower Fufu, Batoka Gorge, and Polihali) show similar patterns of precipitation—high during November through March and lower the rest of the year. Pwalugu exhibits the opposite

Figure 7.1 Annual Cycle of Precipitation for Each Test Project Based on the Historical Record

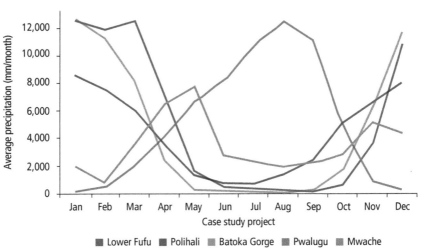

cycle, with peak precipitation during July, August, and September. Mwache has two rainy seasons—in the spring and late fall.

Global climate models suggest a wide range of plausible changes in precipitation in the test project regions (figure 7.2). For all five test projects, however, some climate model projections suggest conditions will get significantly wetter over the coming four to five decades, whereas others suggest that conditions will get significantly drier over the same period.

Each test project uses planning-level models to evaluate project benefits and costs over time under different assumptions about future climate change and other factors. The test projects use the RDM methodology to structure the analysis and identify potentially robust project configurations.

Each study began by evaluating a range of designs under historical climate conditions. This approach is analogous to the approach taken in a standard prefeasibility or feasibility study, and identifies a design that is optimized based on historical climate. This design will not necessarily coincide with the one proposed in the project's feasibility studies, as the latter benefit from a range of information on factors influencing design, broader than those available to the

Figure 7.2 Range of Historical and Annual Projected Precipitation Changes by 2050 for the Five Watersheds, from 121 Climate Projections from the Global Climate Models

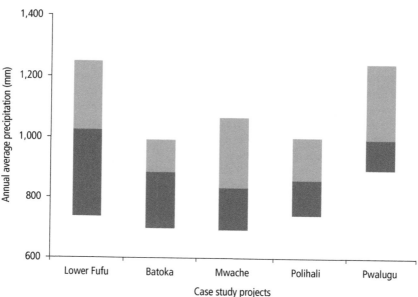

Note: The center line in each bar shows historical average annual precipitation (in millimeters or mm); the top and bottom of each bar show the highest and lowest annual precipitation projection across the 121 climate projections.

study team of the present report. The analyses then evaluate the climate sensitivity of the same design alternatives, or a subset, by evaluating their performance under a broad range of plausible future conditions. These results help identify one or more *robust designs* (i.e., designs capable of delivering acceptable performance under a wide range of climate scenarios). If a new feasibility analysis were to use this approach, it likely would begin with evaluation of the larger set of climate change futures, and not emphasize the historically optimal case.

The next step, trade-off analysis, uses the results from the previous steps to support an assessment of alternative designs. Analysts develop interactive visualizations that highlight the key trade-offs among different designs and their performance across the different futures, including the scenarios that illuminate the key vulnerabilities. At this point in the process, additional scientific information and expert judgment can be incorporated to provide context about the likelihoods of the key scenarios. Stakeholder preferences about different outcomes can be considered along with the analytic results, to help inform the selection of a robust strategy. In many cases, these deliberations identify a design that is preliminary and contains elements that need further evaluation, refinement, or augmentation. This preliminary robust design can then be used as a new starting point for additional iterations through the process. In this way, RDM helps support an ongoing, iterative planning process that can accompany the implementation over time of large and potentially costly design choices.

Table 7.1 provides a summary of the uncertainties used as inputs for the analyses, the project performance metrics, the infrastructure design parameters (effectively, these are climate adaptation levers), and the models used. Each analysis uses a hydrology and water management model (last column) to estimate project inflows and operations (performance metrics in the fourth column) under each climate future (second column) and project design alternative (fifth column). Each test project presented here is based on models developed in the Water Evaluation and Planning (WEAP) system—the system described in chapter 2 and applied throughout the study.

To support the comparisons of alternative project designs on an economic basis, the models developed for each test project estimate the costs of alternative project designs based on the parameters described in each project's prefeasibility or feasibility report. These models, implemented as a spreadsheet, are designed first to reproduce the cost estimates for the feasibility designs. They then adjust costs for different project components based on broad alternative design specifications—for example, higher or lower dam height.

The models use standard engineering relationships to determine material and labor cost variances for different designs. In addition, a variety of parameters were either directly extracted from the summary tables within the feasibility reports or inferred from other presented data: quantities of materials,

Table 7.1 Key Features of the Test Project Analyses

Case study	Climate inputs	Other uncertainties	Performance metrics	Infrastructure design parameters	Models
Lower Fufu Hydropower Project	121 climate futures	None	Hydropower generation Cost of project Levelized cost of hydropower generation	Diversion design flows for two rivers	Hydrology and operations model (WEAP Lower Fufu) Lower Fufu Design and Cost Tool
Batoka Gorge Hydropower Project	121 climate futures	Hydropower revenue price	Hydropower generation Cost of project Levelized cost of hydropower generation NPV for project	Dam height Hydropower capacity Power purchase agreement	Hydrology and operations model (WEAP Batoka) Batoka Project Cost Tool
Mwache Dam and Reservoir Project	121 climate futures	Municipal water demand Economic consequences of shortages	Safe yield of water supply Value of urban and agricultural supply (2020–60) Cost and NPV of project	Dam height and storage	Hydrology and operations model (WEAP Mwache) Mwache Project Cost Tool
Polihali Dam and Conveyance Project	121 climate futures	None	Safe yield from Polihali Dam Cost per unit of safe yield Cost and NPV of project	Dam height and storage Average annual transfer target Guaranteed transfer level	Hydrology and operations model (WEAP Polihali) Polihali Project Cost Tool
Pwalugu Multipurpose Dam Project	121 climate futures	Cost of irrigation development Benefit of irrigation supply	Pwalugu hydropower production Net hydropower generation Irrigation support area Hydropower levelized cost Irrigation and net hydropower value Cost and NPV of project	Dam height and capacity Turbine capacity Irrigation area	Hydrology and operations model (WEAP Pwalugu) Pwalugu Project Cost Tool

Note: NPV = net present value; WEAP = Water Evaluation and Planning.

size of equipment, assumed unit cost of materials or equipment, local economic impacts on unit cost assumptions, and time period for when the cost estimate was relevant. Additional details on the input data for these models are included in online appendix G.[2]

The test projects evaluate the performance of the projects using standard feasibility metrics—such as safe yield, firm yield, and levelized cost of electricity.

In four of the five test projects, a rough economic analysis was performed to illustrate the relative effects of different climate change scenarios (for all but the Lower Fufu). These economic analyses are simplified, because of the limited data, and consider the cost of capital, the timing of accrued assumed costs and benefits, and the assumed value of hydropower and water supply yields. The economic analyses use the net present value (NPV) of the project as the basis for project performance comparisons. Externalities, negative or positive, are not included in the economic analyses.

The economic analyses estimate the future performance of the project from a future construction date through 2050. The simulations for the economic analyses thus are based on fewer years than the safe and firm yield calculations. As a result, designs that are shown to minimize cost based on a 50-year simulation period may be more or less optimal than the same design based on NPV calculations for a shorter period of time.

The study limits the analysis of climate change effects to the economic performance of water infrastructure via changed power production or safe water supply. It does not take into account potential cost effects in construction and maintenance, for example, to deal with changed extreme floods or altered sediment inflow to reservoirs.

Results: Sensitivity and Vulnerability to Climate at the Project Scale

The climate change analyses conducted for the five test projects show that the performance of the project designs can be sensitive to future climate. The design assessed as optimal based on historical climate conditions does not generally perform well across all plausible future climate conditions. In drier futures, smaller facilities yield higher net benefits, as less investment is underutilized during the dry periods. In wetter futures, larger facilities that can better take advantage of high flow periods yield higher net benefits.

The effect of sensitivity to climate change on the performance in hydropower production is initially illustrated by analyses for the Pwalugu and Batoka Gorge projects (figures 7.3 and 7.4).

In the Pwalugu case, climate change may result in up to a 30 percent decrease or a 30 percent increase in average power production for the period up to 2050. The Batoka case also shows significant sensitivity to climate change with up to a 33 percent decrease or a 15 percent increase in average power production. Because of the large size of the Batoka project, this relates to a span on the order of US$4 billion in present value of revenues for the 30-year economic life span between the worst and best scenarios, assuming average levelized cost of power in the Southern African Power Pool.

Figure 7.3 Hydrology and Evaporation Effects on Hydropower Production from the Pwalugu Multipurpose Project across Climate Projections

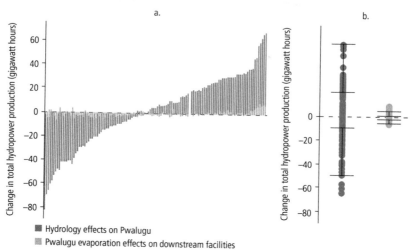

■ Hydrology effects on Pwalugu
▨ Pwalugu evaporation effects on downstream facilities

Note: Results are for dam storage capacity of 4,200 MCM. Each bar (left) and dot (right) corresponds to one of the 145 climate projections. Red bars indicate the net change in hydropower production from hydrology and evaporation effects. Power generation under historical climate is 240 gigawatt hours per year.

The effect of sensitivity to climate change on the performance of the Mwache Dam to deliver safe yields is also prominent. When evaluating across the range of 121 future climate projections, the result is a wide range in safe yields (figure 7.5). Notably, 61 percent of the futures lead to higher safe yields than under the historical conditions, which is consistent with the range in projected precipitation in eastern Kenya.

A deeper review of the test projects indicates that although project performance is potentially sensitive to climate change, the project's economic worthiness is not necessarily in question. That is, the project may have already been designed to be robust to a high degree of climate variability (and in the bargain, to climate change). In some cases, the benefits and revenues of the water infrastructure project are so high that risks for negatively performing projects are low even in extreme future climates, or benefits do not differ significantly across the climate scenarios. It is thus important to distinguish between climate sensitivity and vulnerability. Sensitivity and vulnerability may vary depending on what performance metrics are studied and may be heavily influenced by factors other than climate change (e.g., price and demand for power or water).

Figure 7.4 Mean Batoka Gorge Annual Hydropower Generation versus Mean Annual River Flow across 121 Climate Projections and Historical Climate

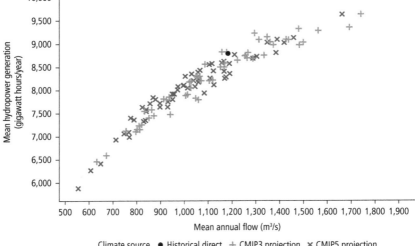

Climate source   ● Historical direct   + CMIP3 projection   × CMIP5 projection

Note: CMIP3 corresponds to the IPCC Fourth Assessment general circulation model (GCM) results. CMIP5 corresponds to the IPCC Fifth Assessment GCM results. m³/s = cubic meters per second.

Figure 7.5 Safe Yield for Mwache Dam across 121 Climate Projections

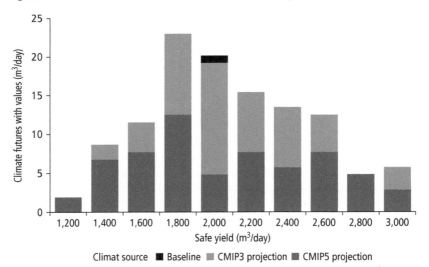

Climat source   ■ Baseline   ■ CMIP3 projection   ■ CMIP5 projection

Note: CMIP3 corresponds to the IPCC Fourth Assessment general circulation model (GCM) results. CMIP5 corresponds to the IPCC Fifth Assessment GCM results. Values are for the 120 million cubic meters (m³) design.

A summary of the vulnerability of projects across climates is provided in figure 7.6, where vulnerability is defined in terms of NPV for project performance for four of the five test projects before adaptations to the designs. The wide range of vulnerability, relative to the historical optimum, suggests that there is great value in conducting the climate "stress tests" described in this chapter for all project designs.

The assessment of possible adaptation measures for the test projects shows that different project designs have considerably different spans of performance across the multiple climate futures. The analysis of regrets for different choices of design for the Lower Fufu in figure 7.7 illustrates how the span differs depending on which design is chosen. For any given climate, regrets are defined as the difference between project performance under the selected design choice, and project performance for the best-performing design alternative for that climate. Regrets can reflect lost revenues (for example, when drier than expected climate reduces hydropower production); or they can reflect lost opportunities (for example, when the opportunity afforded by a wet climate to produce more hydropower is not seized). Figure 7.7, panel a, shows hydropower generation across climates for 11 alternative designs (horizontal axis). Panel b shows the levelized cost performance metric across climates and design options, and panel

Figure 7.6 Summary of Vulnerability of Projects across Climates, before Design Adaptation

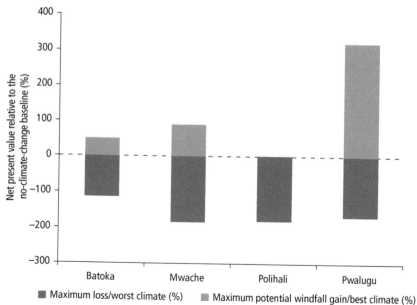

■ Maximum loss/worst climate (%)   ■ Maximum potential windfall gain/best climate (%)

Figure 7.7 Lower Fufu Project: Average Hydropower Generation, Levelized Cost, and Levelized Cost Regret across Design Alternatives and Climate Projections

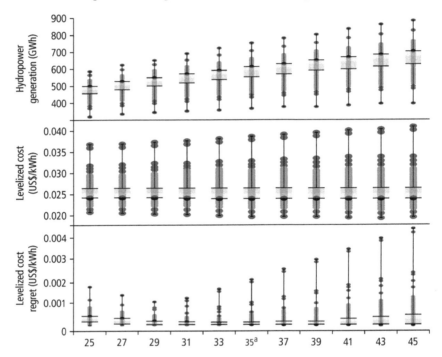

Note: The shaded region indicates the interquartile range (25 to 75 percentile) of performance across climate scenarios; whiskers indicate the full range of results. Levelized costs assume a 5 percent interest rate and 5 percent discount rate. The design alternatives are given as total turbine flow capacity in cubic meters per second (m³/s).
a. The 35 m³/s design is marked to highlight that this is the optimum design based on historical records. The dots in the graphs are climate projections.

c shows levelized cost regrets for the same variants. The three panels illustrate the overall process of the analyses—developing a set of alternative design options, conducting a climate stress test across those options, and assessing the regrets of these alternatives. A criterion for decision making that minimizes the maximum regret would imply the choice of Design 29, because the top of the whisker is lowest for that design in panel c. A criterion to minimize the 75th percentile regret, by contrast, would indicate that Designs 31, 33, and 35 are almost equally favored, because the top of the box (75th percentile outcome) is lowest for those design choices in panel c. These alternative paradigms for robust decision making are discussed in further detail in the next section.

For other test projects, the project team found that with a choice of different designs for the Batoka Gorge project, the maximum regret can be reduced between 60 and 80 percent (depending on regional electricity price levels) compared with the maximum regret at risk if the best design for a historical climate were chosen. Similarly, for the Polihali project, an alternative to the design based on historical climate yields a significant decrease (30 percent) in the maximum regret. In all cases, however, these results are designed to be illustrative only—they do not imply that the choices made in these specific feasibility studies are incorrect or suboptimal. Figure 7.8 illustrates the effect of design adaptations illustrated by the Batoka, Mwache, Polihali, and Pwalugu case studies.

The case studies further showed that designs appropriate for the historical climate may be robust over a wide range of climate futures if the designs are paired with flexibility in the choice of water or power contracts. In particular, for Batoka Gorge, from the point of view of the operation, more nuanced contracts can be used to recoup the costs of larger designs under wet futures while distributing the risks of overbuilding for dry climates to the energy or water consumers.

Figure 7.8 **Potential Economic Benefits That Derive from Adapting Project Design**

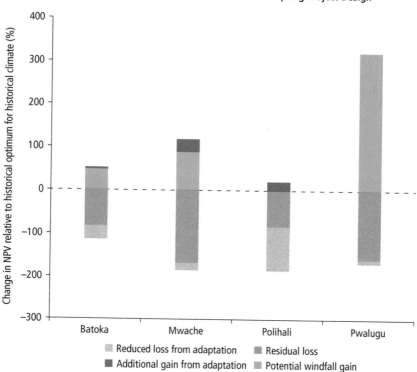

Results: Illustration of Robust Design at the Project Scale

There is no single definition of robustness in the decision making or planning literatures. This study's project-level analysis allowed us to compare the implications of using several alternative criteria. In general, we found that the alternative robustness criteria give similar policy recommendations, although in some cases there are differences that can highlight issues of potential importance to policy makers.

In particular, the analysis highlights the key trade-offs among different designs based on three alternative robustness criteria (table 7.2). All three criteria employ a measure of regret, defined as the difference between the performance of a configuration in some future compared with the performance of the best configuration for that future.

The first criterion is the traditional mini-max regret criterion and is the easiest to implement, but can be unduly influenced by extreme cases. The second is known in the literature as a domain criterion, and is particularly useful when no probabilistic information exists about alternative futures. The third criterion notes that there often exists some probabilistic information, albeit imprecise, regarding the relative likelihood of alternative future conditions. To implement this criterion here, the analysis looks for project designs that satisfice over a restricted range of futures, generally ranges that exclude the most extreme wet or dry climate projections. The analysis can then ask how likely these extreme climate projections would need to be for decision makers to prefer a project design that performs well specifically in these extremes over a design that satisfices over a broader range of futures.

As discussed earlier, the robust choice can differ depending on the decision criteria selected. For example, in figure 7.7, the robust choice according to the first criterion—minimize maximum regret—is Design 29, where the height of the regrets "whisker" in panel c is lowest. Note that this design is 17 percent smaller than the historical optimal design (Design 35). It is smaller primarily to

Table 7.2 Robustness Criteria Used in the Case Studies

Robustness criteria	References
1) Minimize maximum regret over a set of evaluated futures	Savage 1951
2) Satisfice over a wide range of future conditions	Rosenhead 2001; Lempert et al. 2006; Lempert and Collins 2007
3) Satisfice over a wide range of likelihoods for future conditions (implemented here as satisficing over a restricted range of future conditions)	Lempert and Collins 2007; Nassopoulos, Dumas, and Hallegatte 2012

accommodate the two driest climate projections, which are likely an extreme outcome.

The second criterion—satisficing over a wide range of future conditions—is considered in figure 7.9, which shows which designs have low regret for each of the climate projections in terms of the average annual flow. In the figure, the totals indicate for how many futures each design is a low-regret design. In general, smaller designs have lower regret for low-runoff futures and larger designs have lower regret for higher-runoff futures. Using this criterion, Design 37 is the lowest regret over the most climate futures (Design 21). The smallest design shown (Design 25) is low-regret for 10 futures, suggesting that for some particularly dry futures, even smaller designs could be low-regret.

The third robustness criterion—satisficing over a wide range of likelihoods for future conditions—focuses not on the specific futures selected for the analysis, but rather the ranges of uncertainty that affect the choice of design. In this case, the analysis of the specific sample of climate futures identified that annual streamflow is the dominant uncertainty affecting the choice of design. Therefore, this decision criterion identifies the designs that satisfice—have sufficiently low regret—across the range of plausible future annual stream flows of greatest concern.

Figure 7.9 Low-Regret Designs for Each Climate Projection for the Lower Fufu Project

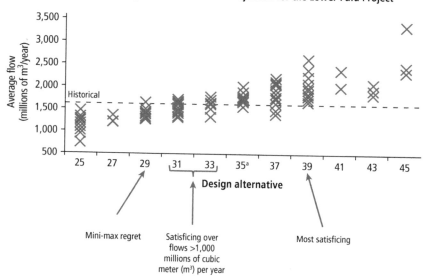

a. The historical optimum is Design 35.

Of the three robustness criteria, the mini-max regret criterion suggests the smallest design—Design 29—because it performs relatively best in the extreme wet and extreme dry climate projections. The second criterion produces the largest design—Design 37—because it performs best over the middle range of stream flows generated by the majority of climate projections in the ensemble. With the third criterion, when the analysis excludes the few driest climate projections, those that generate stream flows less than 1,000 million cubic meters per year (more than a third less than historic), the most robust designs—Designs 31 and 33—are only slightly smaller than the optimal design the model provides for historical conditions (Design 35).

Figure 7.10 provides an illustration of the potential of robust decision making to reduce the regrets of choosing a particular design, when faced with the uncertainty of future climate, for the other four test projects. As indicated in the figure, the robust design in these illustrative case studies reduces regrets substantially for the Batoka, Mwache, and Polihali illustrative calculations, but there are no designs that are able to reduce regrets in the Pwalugu analysis. The lesson is that, if there are few or no effective options for adapting project design, it may not be worth pursuing a robust decision-making analysis. Some level of "screening" analysis, however, may be needed to determine if this result will hold.

Figure 7.10 Potential for Robust Adaptation to Reduce Regrets

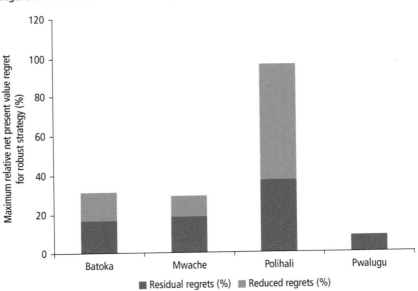

Conclusions

The analyses summarized in this chapter suggest that three broad-based conclusions can be drawn:

- *The performance of project designs can be sensitive to future climate.* Project design defined on the basis of historical climate conditions does not generally perform well across all plausible future climate conditions. In drier futures, smaller facilities yield higher net benefits, as less investment is underutilized during the dry periods. In wetter futures, larger facilities that can better take advantage of high-flow periods yield higher net benefits.

- *Although project performance is sensitive to climate change, the performance may not need to be vulnerable.* In some cases, the benefits and revenues of the water infrastructure project are so high that risks for negatively performing projects are low even in extreme future climates, or benefits do not differ significantly across the climate scenarios. It is thus important to distinguish between climate sensitivity and vulnerability. Sensitivity and vulnerability may vary depending on what performance metrics are studied and may be heavily influenced by factors other than climate change (e.g., price and demand for power or water).

- *Designs appropriate for the historical climate may be robust over a wide range of climate futures if paired with flexibility in the choice of water or power contracts.* From the point of view of the operation, more nuanced contracts can be used to recoup the costs of larger designs under wet futures while distributing the risks of overbuilding for dry climates to the energy or water consumers. RDM methods can be used to evaluate these strategies thoroughly to ensure that improved robustness can be achieved.

These general observations can play out differently for different water infrastructure projects. Figure 7.11 provides a schematic summary of the value of conducting a full climate change vulnerability and robust response option analysis in the feasibility studies for each of the five projects considered here. The projects are compared according to the extent to which (a) the design optimized for historical climate may perform poorly across a range of alternative climates, and (b) the range of design options considered might be combined to yield a design that is robust across this range of climates. For those projects in which the vulnerability is high and the effectiveness of response options is high, further climate change vulnerability and response option analysis would be particularly prudent.

It is essential to note that vulnerability to climate change is a combination of climate sensitivity (physical effect on production or yield) and the financial and

Figure 7.11 Typology of Project Vulnerability and Adaptation Benefits

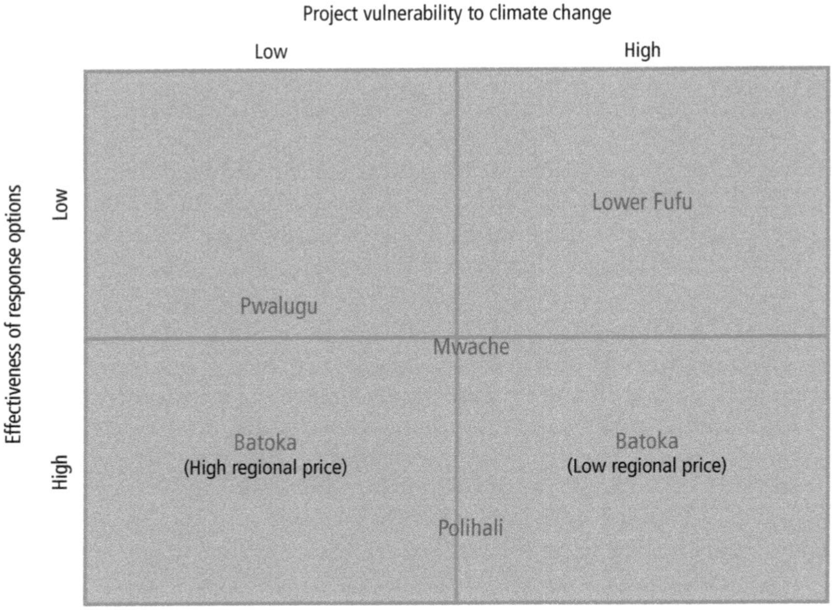

Project vulnerability to climate change

economic conditions. This is illustrated in figure 7.11 by the Batoka Gorge projects being differently vulnerable to climate change depending on the regional price level of electricity. The effectiveness of the response options is directly dependent on the adaptation measures that are available. The positions of the five test projects in figure 7.11 are therefore only valid under the assumptions and limitations applied in this study and should not be considered general for these projects.

The study of the five test projects therefore suggests that the value of conducting a full climate change vulnerability and robust response option analysis may vary from project to project. The results show that for those projects for which the vulnerability is high and the effectiveness of response options is high, the economic gains can be considerable. And although a project may be found to have limited vulnerability to climate change, or the effectiveness of adaptation may be found to be limited, conducting analyses such as those illustrated here, to gain this knowledge, would be a useful part of the technical design and financial solutions of the project.

Lessons Learned and Insights for Broader Application

Many African countries plan to make significant investments in water infrastructure under conditions where hard-to-predict future changes in climate are expected to have significant impacts on the performance of that infrastructure. This study presents five case studies of projects in the water sector to analyze how project designs might be adjusted to make them more robust to potential climate change. The analyses for the five test projects show how the effects of climate change can be mitigated by suitably choosing certain design parameters (e.g., height of dams) so as to manage the effects on a single performance indicator (typically project NPV). The analysis is illustrative, since in reality the final design will be defined on the basis of several performance indicators (not just NPV), handled through a multi-criteria analysis. The more important point here was to demonstrate how the relevant project design parameters can be defined (whatever the decision criteria) on the basis of not just one future hydrological regime, but many possible ones, as each of the uncertain climate scenarios implies a hydrological regime that can be very different from the historical one.

The case studies are all screening analyses, which have focused on economic performance and include important simplifications, and are thus not intended to provide definitive conclusions regarding alternative project designs. However, the order of magnitude of the NPV regrets (underperformance or missed opportunities) indicated by these studies shows that climate change is likely important to take into account when planning and designing large water infrastructure projects if economic performance is an important decision factor. These large regrets need not be a show-stopper if the revenues are still sufficient to give positive economic performance in most climate futures, but may be an opportunity to improve the economic value of the water services. The information on regrets over climate change futures, depending on the developer's preference, can be used to hedge negative NPVs or to wager on higher deliveries by increased investments.

This study demonstrates an approach for climate change vulnerability and response option screening analyses that can be incorporated into feasibility studies to inform the final conceptual design. The screening analysis can be expanded to include increasing the level of detail if climate change proves to be important for the project. A fundamental part of the screening analysis is to understand the most important performance metrics that will determine the final design of the infrastructure project. The key metrics for the design of large water infrastructure are not always just related to financial or economic performance, and may include a wide range of performance metrics. The five test cases presented in this report largely focus on a single metric for

each project. But in general such screening analyses could address the performance of a range of essential metrics. However, such multi-attribute RDM
analyses could become complicated. In noncomplex, single-purpose projects,
the screening analyses will be able to encompass a full RDM analysis for the
ultimate design, with many climate futures. In many cases, however, the
screening analysis will be conducted early in the feasibility study process to
guide the choice of a few representative design hydrologies, which could then
be used to inform the choice of a detailed technical design that is robust across
those hydrologies.

The modeling components required for climate change analysis consist of
the following:

- A simple project design and cost model that can reproduce any existing cost
  estimates from a prefeasibility study and estimate how costs would vary with
  alternative design specifications. If the complexity of the design precludes
  the development of a simple design and cost model, several estimates of
  alternative designs could be developed with the more detailed tools.

- A set of downscaled climate projections for the project's relevant geographic
  region.

- A hydrologic model of the relevant region, calibrated to local observational
  records and linked to climate projections, that can estimate project inflows
  and operations for alternative design specifications.

The requisite sets of climate projections have become increasingly available.
Appropriate hydrological modeling platforms, such as the WEAP system used
for these case studies, have also become increasingly available and can be calibrated with the same data utilized in feasibility studies. This project has generated a set of project design and cost models embodied in Excel spreadsheets that
can be used as templates for a wide range of alternative projects.

Once the modeling components have been assembled, the RDM analysis
requires two types of enabling software. First, analysts require scripts for the
water modeling and project design and cost modeling software to run the models over many cases for an appropriate experimental design. This project used
such scripts designed to run with the WEAP software and with spreadsheet
models. Second, analysts require software for visualization and analyzing the
resulting database of model runs.

With these software tools in place, analysts can conduct studies such as
those described in this report by structuring the decision problem using an
elicitation framework called "XLRM"—for uncertainties (X), policy levers (L),
relationships among factors (R), and measures of policy performance (M).
Analysts can then run many cases of the models, as suggested by the XLRM
framework, input the resulting database into Tableau, and develop

visualizations similar to those displayed in this report. These visualizations can provide the trade-off curves using the three robustness criteria employed here.

At present, sample scripts for running multiple cases of WEAP, a spreadsheet design and cost model, and Tableau visualizations can be made available to and adapted by other analysts for use in other projects. In the future, the World Bank might consider developing training programs and web-based tools to facilitate widespread use of these analyses.

This report was conducted by an independent research team, using data from prefeasibility studies to conduct screening analyses to inform future feasibility studies. Preferably, the screening analyses should be conducted as part of the feasibility consortium, because to make the analyses effective requires seamless access to input data from a broad spectrum of experts and guidance from experienced dam engineers involved in the project. The experience of this work has clearly shown the difficulties of making relevant analyses without direct access to the feasibility consultant.

This study focused on uncertainties in project performance caused by climate change. The RDM-based method can also be used to address other critical uncertainties relevant to the design of large hydropower and water supply infrastructure. For instance, several of the case studies—e.g., Batoka Gorge and Mwache—showed that the economics of projects of this type could be highly sensitive to the price of power and the demand for water. The Pwalugu case study highlights the importance of development on downstream water uses. The level of upstream development may be a critical uncertainty that is equally or even more important than climate in many contexts.

Overall, the results presented in this report are encouraging. They indicate that climate change data, despite their uncertainty, can be incorporated in a systematic way into the technical design of water infrastructure projects with likely net economic benefits for the developer and customers as the end result. Many challenges remain to make such integration possible on a regular basis, considering data access and time and budget constraints, but these could be overcome if practitioners work across sector and disciplinary boundaries, and support is given from policy makers to raise the awareness and requirements of taking climate change into account in infrastructure planning.

Notes

1. Some details of the analyses might nonetheless be useful to some readers. Please contact Raffaello Cervigni of the World Bank (rcervigni@worldbank.org) to request additional information.
2. Appendix G is available online at https://openknowledge.worldbank.org /handle/10986/21875.

References

Consult 4 Consortium and SEED Consult. 2007. Lesotho Highlands Water Project–Consulting Services for the Feasibility Study for Phase II: Main Report.

Lempert, R. J., and M. T. Collins. 2007. "Managing the Risk of Uncertain Threshold Responses: Comparison of Robust, Optimum, and Precautionary Approaches." *Risk Analysis: An Official Publication of the Society for Risk Analysis* 27: 1009–26.

Lempert, R. J., D. G. Groves, S. W. Popper, and S. C. Bankes. 2006. "A General, Analytic Method for Generating Robust Strategies and Narrative Scenarios." *Management Science* 52: 514–28.

Nassopoulos, H., P. Dumas, and S. Hallegatte. 2012. "Adaptation to an Uncertain Climate Change: Cost Benefit Analysis and Robust Decision Making for Dam Dimensioning." *Climatic Change* 114: 497–508.

Norconsult. 1996. "Lower Fufu Hydropower Project: Pre-Feasibility Study, Final Report, Volume 1, Technical / Economic Aspects."

Rosenhead, J. 2001. "Robust Analysis: Keeping Your Options Open." In *Rational Analysis for a Problematic World Revisited: Problem Structuring Methods for Complexity, Uncertainty, and Conflict*, edited by J. Rosenhead and J. Mingers. Chichester, UK: John Wiley & Sons.

Savage, L. J. 1951. "The Theory of Statistical Decision." *Journal of the American Statistical Association* 46: 55–67.

Tahal Group. 2013. "Mombasa Water Supply Master Plan."

Volta River Authority. 1993. "White Volta Development Scheme, Prefeasibility Study Report."

Zambezi River Authority. 1993. "Batoka Gorge Hydropower Feasibility Study."

Chapter 8

Recommendations

Raffaello Cervigni, Fatima Denton, and Rikard Liden

This report has produced a set of results at the regional, basin, and project scales that provide a strong impetus for modifying business-as-usual infrastructure planning and design in Africa to incorporate climate change explicitly. This chapter summarizes the findings and gives suggestions on how to achieve the proposed change in infrastructure development practice.

Need for a Paradigm Shift in How Large Infrastructure Is Planned and Designed

While infrastructure development is vital to Africa's growth, there is a high potential that climate change will offset or reduce the benefits of such infrastructure. Climate change forecasts for the Sub-Saharan Africa region suggest increases in temperature in the range of 1 to 2 degrees Celsius by 2050, but precipitation forecasts vary widely by location and time period, and suggest that drier and wetter futures are plausible. The seven basins in this study include climate forecasts that are drier than history, with reduced generation of hydropower (leading to higher prices for electric power and higher greenhouse gas emissions from fossil electric energy that must be deployed to replace the lost hydropower) and lower levels of irrigation water supply (leading to reduced agricultural production and a greater need for imported food). All seven basins also include climate forecasts that are wetter than history, which lead to increased productivity of hydropower and irrigation infrastructure. However, this windfall gain in productivity in a wetter future may not result in economic gains for society without prior investments to utilize it.

Adaptation has great potential to reduce the negative impacts of climate change, but the planning and design of infrastructure in Africa are still conducted largely without taking climate change into account. At the basin and project levels, the report demonstrates that adapting infrastructure planning and design ex ante has great potential to reduce climate change impacts on infrastructure in drier futures, and to take better advantage of higher water availability in wetter futures. The results for the seven river basins and five specific pipeline projects indicate that the benefits of adaptation through alternative designs are significant in economic terms. However, climate change is in most cases not properly integrated in project design and evaluation. This report suggests that failing to adjust designs ex ante to improve infrastructure performance over a range of climate futures may be an economic loss for society in the long term.

Although not yet mainstreamed, there are data and methodologies for including climate change ex ante in the planning and design stage of power and water infrastructure. There is thus no longer any excuse for not taking climate change into account for river basins and project designs in Africa. The results of this study are entirely based on globally available input data, open source software, and methodologies well-developed in the relevant literature. Although the format of these data and the complexity of the models still require extensive expert input at some stages of the analysis, the basic data and methodology exist for taking climate change into account at an early stage of river basin planning and project design.

The use of methodology similar to that applied in this report has been documented in the scientific literature and recent projects and is replicable. In particular, at the project level, this report describes screening analyses that require only climate projections, relatively simple spreadsheet models, and easily constructed hydrological models linked to those projections. Such screening analyses should thus be relatively straightforward to implement for most proposed projects. In those cases in which a screening analysis suggests the need for further analysis, this report suggests methods that might be adopted by the engineering consultants conducting the project feasibility and prefeasibility studies.

At the basin level, this study employs the type of models commonly used for basin-level planning. Such models, combined with libraries of climate projections, are sufficient to carry out the basin-level vulnerability analyses described in this report. However, calculating robust adaptations involves the comparison of optimal basin plans for each of several climate projections (as a key step toward identifying basin plans that are robust across the different projections) and currently requires a level of technical sophistication generally confined to research organizations. In addition, the need to evaluate simultaneously the potential effects of climate change on water and energy infrastructure increases the difficulty of this optimization step. Estimating robust adaptations thus requires technical capabilities that at present are not yet widely available. Nonetheless, the methods described in this report for stress testing existing basin plans over a wide range of climate futures are accessible to many African basin authorities.

It is therefore high time for a paradigm shift, a change of mind-set among planners and decision makers, for how water and power infrastructure shall be planned in Africa. With the proven high impacts of climate change on future water and power infrastructure in Africa illustrated by this report, it is essential that climate change is considered as an important factor for planning and design. The Program for Infrastructure Development in Africa is essential for Africa's growth and can give even larger bearings if implemented in ways that will make it resilient to climate change. But this will require a change of mind-set among key players—engineers, financiers, and decision makers— and incentives for upfront investments in ex ante preparation studies and adaptive design.

Toward a Paradigm Shift: Recommendations for Short-Term Action

Although climate change impacts in the mid-21st century may seem far away, they are going to be very real during the life span of the infrastructure that is planned now and will be built within the coming decade. If the impacts are not taken into account now, there is a considerable risk that the next generation of power and water infrastructure in Africa will be locked into designs that could turn out to be inadequate for the climate of the future, and costly or impossible to modify later. But properly taking climate impacts into consideration requires a major paradigm shift, away from consolidated behavior and practices. Because such a paradigm shift is likely to have a considerable gestation time, the time to act is now, with priority assigned to the following selected areas of interventions.

1. *Develop technical guidelines on the integration of climate change into the planning and design of infrastructure in climate-sensitive sectors.*
The current technical practice in the engineering community, which tends to use the historical climate as a guide for project planning and design, is solidly anchored in more than 100 years of experience. To overcome the understandable resistance in moving away from such practice, there is a need to develop new technical standards, reflecting the consensus of the relevant professional communities.

A multistakeholder technical working group could be established, to develop voluntary technical guidelines on how to apply the notions of climate resilience, discussed at length in this report, to real-life infrastructure planning and design. The group would include representatives from the development community and relevant professional organizations in the engineering and consulting industries—which could be mobilized through vehicles such as the International Commission on Large Dams and public sector stakeholders at the regional (e.g., the New Partnership for Africa's Development) and national levels. The work would build on the efforts recently undertaken by the African Development Bank, World Bank, the International Finance Corporation, and various other development agencies.[1] The work would focus on screening projects for climate risks, expanding projects to address more directly the question of how to modify planning and project design once a program or a project has been found to be sensitive to climate change.

In the short term (six months to one year), the group could produce generic guidance on topics such as reference, historical climate, and climate change scenarios and, at subsequent intervals of 8 to 12 months, sector-specific guidance for key project types, such as hydropower, irrigation, water supply, road transport, etc.

2. Promote an open data knowledge repository for climate-resilient infrastructure development.

To bring down the cost of the analysis needed to integrate climate considerations into infrastructure development, there is a need to establish common data sources (on climate projections, hydrology, standard construction costs, etc.) that could be made available to the public on open data platforms and updated periodically as new information from the scientific and practitioner communities becomes available. There are already similar platforms (including the World Bank's Climate Change Knowledge Portal) that provide opportunities for focusing future efforts toward production and dissemination of data of particular operational relevance for project planning and design. To ensure the credibility of the information provided, suitable vetting mechanisms should be identified (for example, in collaboration with the United Nations Framework Convention on Climate Change secretariat), so that users will have confidence that the data reflect the latest advances of climate science, hydrology, engineering, etc.

3. Establish an Africa climate-resilience project preparation facility.

Building on the seed resources made available for the present study, development organizations could mobilize funds to establish a facility that would provide technical assistance for the systematic integration of climate change in the planning and design of Africa's infrastructure. Although eventually climate resilience analysis should become a regular part of program and project preparation, experience on the ground is limited and technical capacity is scarce; as a result, it would make sense to have an applied knowledge hub, which could provide technical assistance services across the continent for the assessment of climate impacts and particularly for the analysis of adaptation options in project design (including assessment of contracts of service). The facility could have different windows to cater to the specific needs of different sectors or different stages of the infrastructure development cycle. For example, there could be

- A window to support the development of climate-resilient master plans or other similar planning instruments at broad scales (such as river basins, power pools, transport corridors, etc.)
- A window to support the inclusion of climate sensitivity assessments in the preparation of individual projects.

The facility should have adequate trust fund resources, so as not to discourage potential users from accessing its services. It would maintain a small core staff of full-time professionals and a larger roster of part-time experts, who could be deployed to support project developers in the formulation of adequate terms of reference for the inclusion of climate change in prefeasibility and feasibility studies, as well as providing quality assurance services and supervision of the work carried out by third-party consultants. The facility could also serve as a mechanism for exchange and dissemination of practical knowledge on the technical aspects of integrating climate change into project preparation and design, through conferences, websites, technical publications, etc.

4. Launch training programs for climate-resilient infrastructure professionals.

To ensure adequate strengthening of the technical skills that are required to enhance the climate resilience of infrastructure, one or more training programs could be established for professionals involved in the planning, design, and operation of climate-sensitive infrastructure. These could include technical staff of relevant public sector entities (e.g., ministries of water, power, and transport; river basin organizations; and power pools) as well as other professionals in the academic community and the private sector.

5. Set up an observatory on climate-resilient infrastructure development in Africa.

Integration of climate concerns into infrastructure development is a process that will not happen overnight. It will require sustained effort across disciplines, sectors, and levels of decision making. To ensure that the work at the technical level discussed above on methodology, data, project preparation, and training retains visibility and links with the policy level of decision making, it would be important to establish a forum where the progress made is monitored, existing or new challenges are discussed, and policy and financing solutions are identified.

An observatory for climate-resilient infrastructure development could be established, for example, as part of the Infrastructure Consortium for Africa, which is a key platform to catalyze donor and private sector financing of infrastructure projects and programs in Africa, and which already includes climate-resilient infrastructure in its list of priority topics.

The observatory could keep track of programs and projects featuring significant assessments of climate impacts and adaptation options; monitor trends in financing for climate-resilient infrastructure; help identify the technical, informational, financing, and institutional bottlenecks that prevent progress in integrating climate consideration into infrastructure development; and promote a high-level dialogue on possible solutions among decision makers in Africa's national and regional organizations and the international development community.

Note

1. See, for example, the August 2014 news story, "World Bank Policies Include Screening for Climate Risks," at http://www.worldbank.org/en/news/feature/2014/08/04/world-band-policies-include-screening-climate-risks.

Index

Boxes, figures, maps, notes, and tables are indicated by *b*, *f*, *m*, *n*, and *t*, respectively, following the page numbers.